DISPATCHES FROM THE EDGE

DISPATCHES FROM THE EDGE

A Memoir of War, Disasters, and Survival

ANDERSON COOPER

HarperLargePrint
An Imprint of HarperCollins*Publishers*

HarperCollins books may be purchased for educational, business, or sales promotional use. For information, please write: Special Markets Department, HarperCollins Publishers, 10 East 53rd Street, New York, NY 10022.

All photographs courtesy of the author unless otherwise noted.

FIRST HARPER LARGE PRINT EDITION

Printed on acid-free paper

Library of Congress Cataloging-in-Publication Data is available upon request.

ISBN-10: 0-06-113805-3
ISBN-13: 978-0-06-113805-8

06 07 08 09 10 BVG/RRD 10 9 8 7 6 5 4 3 2 1

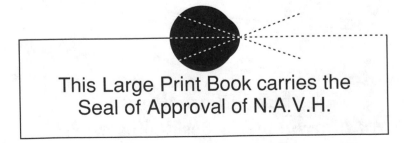

This Large Print Book carries the
Seal of Approval of N.A.V.H.

To my mom and dad, and the spark of
recognition that brought them together

Contents

Introduction

I was ten when my father died, and before that moment, that slap of silence that reset the clock, I can't remember much. There are some things, of course—fractals, shards of memory, sharp as broken glass. I remember an old globe that sat on the table by my bed. I must have been five or six. It was a present from my mother, who'd received it from the author Isak Dinesen, long after she'd written **Out of Africa.**

When I couldn't sleep, I'd touch the globe, trace the contours of continents in the dark. Some nights my small fingers would hike the ridges of Everest, or struggle to reach the summit of Kilimanjaro. Many times, I rounded the Horn of Africa, more than once my ship foundering on rocks off the Cape of Good Hope. The globe was covered with names of nations that no longer exist:

Tanganyika, Siam, the Belgian Congo, Ceylon. I dreamed of traveling to them all.

I didn't know who Isak Dinesen was, but I'd seen her photograph in a delicate gold frame in my mother's bedroom: her face hidden by a hunter's hat, an Afghan hound crouching by her side. To me she was a mysterious figure from my mother's past, just one of many.

My mother's name is Gloria Vanderbilt, and long before I ever got into the news business, she was making headlines. She was born in 1924 to a family of great wealth, and early on discovered its limits. When she was fifteen months old her father died, and for years afterward, she was shuttled about from continent to continent, her mother always moving off into unseen rooms, preparing for parties and evenings on the town. At ten my mother became the center of a highly publicized custody battle. My mother's powerful aunt Gertrude Vanderbilt Whitney was able to convince a New York court that my mother's mother was unfit. It was during the Depression, and the trial was a tabloid obsession. The court took my mother away from her mother and the Irish nurse she truly loved, and handed her over to Whitney who soon sent her away to boarding school.

My brother and I knew none of this as children,

of course, but we'd sometimes seen a look in our mother's eyes, a slight dilation of the pupil, a hint of pain and fear. I didn't know what it meant until after my father died. I glanced at myself in the mirror and saw the same look staring back at me.

———————

As a boy looking at that globe, I grew up believing, as most people do, that the earth is round. Smoothed like a stone by thousands of years of evolution and revolution. Whittled by time. Scraped by space. I thought that all the nations and oceans, the rivers and valleys, were already mapped out, named, explored. But in truth, the world is constantly shifting: shape and size, location in space. It's got edges and chasms, too many to count. They open up, close, reappear somewhere else. Geologists may have mapped out the planet's tectonic plates—hidden shelves of rock that grind, one against the other, forming mountains, creating continents—but they can't plot the fault lines that run through our heads, divide our hearts.

The map of the world is always changing; sometimes it happens overnight. All it takes is the blink of an eye, the squeeze of a trigger, a sudden gust of wind. Wake up and your life is perched on a precipice; fall asleep, it swallows you whole.

None of us likes to believe our lives are so precarious. In 2005, however, we were reminded just how quickly things can change. The year began with the tsunami and came to a close with Hurricane Katrina and its aftermath. There were wars and famine, and other disasters, natural and man-made.

As a correspondent and anchor for CNN, I spent much of 2005 reporting from the front lines in Sri Lanka and New Orleans, Africa and Iraq. This book is about what I saw and experienced, and how it crystallized much of what I'd previously learned and lived through in conflicts and countries long since forgotten.

For years I tried to compartmentalize my life, distance myself from the world I was reporting on. This year, however, I realized that that is not possible. In the midst of tragedy, the memories of moments, forgotten feelings, began to feed off one another. I came to see how woven together these disparate fragments really are: past and present, personal and professional, they shift back and forth again and again. Everyone is connected by the same strands of DNA.

I've been a journalist for fifteen years now, and have reported on some of the worst situations on earth: Somalia, Rwanda, Bosnia, Iraq. I've seen more dead bodies than I can count, more horror and hatred than I can remember, yet I'm still surprised by what I discover in the far reaches of our planet, the truths revealed in the dwindling light of day, when everything else has been stripped away, exposed, raw as a gutted shark on a fisherman's pier. The farther you go, however, the harder it is to return. The world has many edges, and it's very easy to fall off.

———

The week after my father died, I saw one of those old Jacques Cousteau documentaries. It was about sharks. I learned that they have to keep moving in order to live. It's the only way they can breathe. Forward motion, constantly forcing water through their gills. I wanted to live on the **Calypso,** be part of Cousteau's red-capped crew. I imagined myself swimming slowly alongside a Great White, my hand resting lightly on its cold, silver steel skin. I used to dream of its sleek torpedo body silently swaying through pitch black seas, never resting, always in motion. Some nights I still do.

Hurtling across oceans, from one conflict to the next, one disaster to another, I sometimes believe it's motion that keeps me alive as well. I hit the ground running: truck gassed up, camera rolling—"locked and loaded, ready to rock," as a soldier in Iraq once said to me. There's nothing like that feeling. Your truck screeches to a halt, you leap out, the camera resting on the space between your shoulder and neck. You run toward what everyone else is running from, believing your camera will somehow protect you, not really caring if it doesn't. All you want to do is get it, feel it, be in it. The images frame themselves sometimes, the action flows right through you. Keep moving, keep cool, stay alive, force air through your lungs, oxygen into your blood. Keep moving. Keep cool. Stay alive.

I didn't always feel this way. When I started reporting I was twenty-four, and didn't mind waiting for weeks in dingy African hotels. I was on my own with just a home video camera and a fake press pass. I wanted to be a war correspondent but couldn't get a job. In Nairobi, I practically moved into the Ambassadeur Hotel. It was across the street from the Hilton, but a world away. During the day, the second-floor lounge filled with evangelical Christians singing, "Jesus, God is very, very wonderful," while outside, on the street, a man with shiny, steel hooks for hands and pale plastic prostheses for arms waved wildly in the air screaming passages from the Old Testament. At night, the bar opened, and sweating waiters in red jackets served tall glasses of Tusker beer, weaving between black businessmen and prostitutes in shiny emerald dresses. I was alone and lost, clinging to a routine. Lunch at noon. Dinner at six. Weeks passed, and I just waited.

By the time I was twenty-five, it had all changed. I had a job, a salary. I was being paid to go to wars. It had taken me nearly a year of shooting stories, and of hard travel, but I was finally a foreign correspondent. The more I saw, however, the more I needed to see. I tried to settle down back home in Los Angeles, but I missed that feeling, that rush. I went to see a doctor about it. He told me I should slow down for a while, take a break. I just nodded and left, booked a flight out that day. It didn't seem possible to stop.

Working overseas, traversing front lines, I felt the

air hum. Neutrons and protons collided about. I could feel them move through me. No barrier between life and death, just one small step, one foot in front of the other. I wasn't one of those adrenaline cowboys I'd run into in some Third World cul-de-sac. I wasn't looking to get shot at, wasn't looking to take chances. I just didn't let risks get in the way. There was no place I wouldn't go.

Coming home meant coming down. It was easier to stay up. I'd return home to piles of bills and an empty refrigerator. Buying groceries, I'd get lost—too many aisles, too many choices; cool mist blowing over fresh fruit; paper or plastic; cash back in return? I wanted emotion but couldn't find it here, so I settled for motion.

Out at night, weaving through traffic, looking for trouble, I'd lose myself in crowds. Gaggles of girls with fruit-colored drinks talked about face products and film production. I'd see their lips move, look at their snapshot smiles and highlighted hair. I didn't know what to say. I'd look down at my boots and see bloodstains.

The more I was away, the worse it got. I'd come back and couldn't speak the language. Out there the pain was palpable; you breathed it in the air. Back here, no one talked about life and death. No one seemed to understand. I'd go to movies, see friends, but after a couple days I'd catch myself reading plane schedules, looking for something, someplace to go: a bomb in Afghanistan, a flood in Haiti. I'd become a predator, endlessly gliding in saltwater seas, searching for the scent of blood.

I recently saw a documentary about sharks on the Discovery Channel. Scientists had found a species of shark, a deep-water one, that didn't have to keep moving to stay alive. It can breathe lying still. It can rest. I find that hard to believe.

Tsunami
WASHED AWAY

Small waves, one after the other, lap the shore. Two Sri Lankan villagers walk along the water's edge, searching for bodies washed up by the tide. They come every morning, leave without answers. Some days they find nothing. Today there's a torn shoe and a piece of broken fence.

I'm standing in a pile of rubble. Beneath me the ground seems to move, twisting and turning in on itself. It takes a moment for my eyes to adjust. The ground isn't moving at all. It's maggots, thousands of them. Writhing, squirming, they feast on some unseen flesh. Nearby, a dog with low-hanging teats and a face smeared with blood scavenges for scraps. She steps carefully among scattered bricks, tourist snapshots, china plates, the flotsam and jetsam of life before the wave.

It took centuries for the pressure to build. Subtle shifts, grinding force. Long ago, a thousand miles east of Sri Lanka, more than fifteen miles below the surface of the Indian Ocean, two gigantic shelves of rock, tectonic plates, pressed against each other—the rim of what scientists call the India Plate began to push underneath the Burma Plate. Something had to give. At nearly one minute before 8:00 A.M., the morning after Christmas, 2004, the force of the compression explodes along a section of rock some one hundred miles off the west coast of Sumatra. A fault line more than seven hundred miles long violently rips open and a shelf of rock and sediment thrusts upward fifty feet, unleashing an explosion of energy so powerful it alters the rotation of the earth. It is one of the strongest earthquakes in recorded history.

Shock waves pulse in all directions, displacing millions of tons of water, creating giant undersea waves. A tsunami. A ship on the surface of the sea would barely have noticed, detecting perhaps some slight swells no more than two feet high. But underneath, out of sight, churning walls of water extend from the ocean's bottom to the surface, pushing outward. The water moves fast, five hundred miles per hour—the speed of a commercial jetliner.

It takes eight minutes after the earthquake begins for the sonic signals to reach the Pacific Tsunami Warning Center, in Hawaii. The thin needle of a seismograph suddenly springs to life, rapidly scribbling side to side, signaling an alarm. It's already too late. Eight minutes later, at approximately 8:15 A.M., in Banda Aceh, Sumatra, the first of several massive walls of water explodes onto shore. In the next two hours, tsunami waves strike ten other countries. More than two hundred thousand people will die.

In New York, 2005 begins in a blizzard. A hurricane of confetti and light. At the stroke of midnight, I'm standing on a platform in the center of Times Square. I'm about sixty feet off the ground, and below, on the streets all around me, are people—hundreds of thousands of revelers packed shoulder to shoulder behind barricades set up by police. The crowd is cheering. I see their mouths are open, their hands waving in the air, but I can't hear them. Both my ears are plugged with wireless headphones connecting me to a control room several blocks away. I hear only the hiss of the satellite transmission and a thin pulse of blood throbbing in my ears.

It's a strange way to start 2005. We've been covering the tsunami around the clock this week, and each day brings new details, new horrors. There's been talk of canceling the celebrations, but in the end it's decided that the show will go on.

I've always hated New Year's Eve. When I was ten, I lay on the floor of my room with my brother, watching on TV as the crowd in Times Square counted down the remaining seconds of 1977. My father was in the intensive care unit at New York Hospital. He'd had a series of heart attacks, and in a few days would undergo bypass surgery. My brother and I were terrified, but too scared to speak with each other about it. We watched, silent, numb, as the giant crystal ball made its slow descent. It all seemed so frightening: the screaming crowds, the frigid air, not knowing if our father would live through the new year.

I grew up in New York but never went to see the ball drop until I volunteered to cover it for CNN. For most New Yorkers, the idea of going anywhere

near Times Square on New Year's Eve is incon-
ceivable. It's like eating at Tavern On The Green;
the food may be tasty, but it's best left to out-of-
towners.

I've always thought that New Year's Eve is proof
that human beings are essentially optimistic crea-
tures. Despite hundreds of years of pathetic parties and hellish hangovers, we continue to cling to
the notion that it's possible to have fun on that
night. It's not. There's too much pressure, too
many expectations, too few bathrooms.

The truth is, I began volunteering to work on
New Year's Eve as a way to avoid having to do
something social. This is my second time covering the Times Square festivities, and I've actually
begun to enjoy it. There aren't many opportuni-
ties in this city to feel part of a community. We
scuttle about the streets each day, individual at-
oms occasionally running into one another but
rarely coalescing to form a whole. In Times Square,
however, as the ball descends and the crowd
cheers, New York becomes a very different place,
a place of pure feeling.

When midnight arrives, the air explodes into a
solid mass, a swirl of colored confetti that seems
to hang suspended in space. For several minutes I
am not expected to say anything. The pictures take

over. The cameras pan the streets, wide shots and close-ups; people sing and shout. I take the headphones out of my ears and am surrounded by the waves of sound. The air seems to shake, and for a few brief moments I feel part of something larger, not lost in the crowd but swept up by it, buoyed by the emotion, the energy, the joyful pandemonium. It overwhelms my defenses, my hard-won cynicism. The past gives way to the present, and I give myself up to it—the possibilities, the potential.

It doesn't last long. By 12:30, it's over. I thank the viewers for watching, and the broadcast ends; the lights go out. The crowds have already dispersed, pushed along by tired police and armies of street sweepers cleaning up debris. I shake hands with the cameramen, and crew, wish everyone a happy new year. There are genuine smiles, and jokes. We pause for pictures, arms around one another—quick snapshots I'll never see. A few minutes later I walk home alone. I have a flight to Sri Lanka that takes off in the morning. I still have to pack. There's no point in sleeping.

When I first started reporting, in the early 1990s, I used to experience anxiety attacks before heading overseas. Packing bags, sitting on a plane, breathing in all that recycled air and anticipation, I felt like an astronaut floating in space—untethered, unmoored. Whatever thin bonds I'd established back home, whatever delicate connections, I'd willingly severed. I used to think that these anxiety attacks were just part of the process—a midair metamorphosis I had to go through the closer I got to the edge. They were a warning, of course, but it took me years to understand this.

At dawn I board the plane, the first of several I'll take to get to Sri Lanka. When I sit down, the flight attendant tells me I still have confetti in my hair.

Sometimes I wonder if I'm the person I was born to be, if the life I've lived really is the one I was meant to, or if it is some half life, a mutation engineered by loss, cobbled together by the will to survive.

My father's name was Wyatt Cooper. He was born in Quitman, Mississippi, a small town hit hard by the Depression, which started just two years after his birth. His family was poor, his father was a farmer, though by all accounts not a very diligent one.

My father was a born storyteller. As a child, he was often asked to give sermons at Quitman's First Baptist Church when the preacher was out of town.

He wanted to be an actor from the time he was little, but in Quitman during the Depression that didn't seem like a very realistic goal.

"Listen to me, boy, and I'll make you the youngest goddamn governor this state's ever had," my grandfather would bellow at my dad. But my father had no interest in his father's far-fetched political plans.

Whenever he could save up money, he'd hitch a ride into Quitman and see movies at the Majestic, the only theater in town. **The Philadelphia Story** played there; so did **Gone With the Wind.** Films showed for only a day or two, but my father tried to see them all. He'd save the ticket stubs in a scrapbook.

Eventually he left Mississippi and worked as an actor in Hollywood and Italy, did stage productions, and took bit parts in TV dramas and cigarette ads, but his career never really took off. He found more success as a screenwriter, working at Twentieth Century Fox.

My parents met at a dinner party. Their backgrounds could not have been more different. My father had never been married and had a large clan of brothers and sisters and a mother whom he adored. My mother was an only child estranged from her mother, and her third marriage, to director Sidney Lumet, had just ended. In each other, however, they recognized something—a desire for family, a need to belong. "There was something about his eyes," my mother later told me. "We were from very different worlds, but he understood me better than anyone else ever had." They were married just before Christmas, 1964. One year later my brother, Carter, was born. I came along two years after that.

My mother is a remarkably talented artist, and when I was young she began to design home furnishings. She then moved into fashion, and produced an enormously successful line of designer jeans and perfume. My father was working on a book and writing magazine articles. He usually wrote from home, and sometimes, late at night, if I couldn't sleep, I'd go into his study and curl up in his lap like a puppy, my arms wrapped around his neck, my ear pressed against his chest. I could always fall asleep listening to the beat of his heart.

I'm unable to sleep on the flight to Sri Lanka. It's nearly a week since the tsunami struck and already I fear I've missed the story—the bodies and the burials, the emotion of the moment. Like a raw recruit who thinks the war will end before he sees action, I wanted to go the minute this happened. It's the way it always is: find the worst-off place and plunge in head first. It sounds strange, ghoulish, perhaps, but it's the truth. I want to be there, want to see it. Once I am there, however, I've quickly seen enough.

On the plane the flight attendant asks a Sri Lankan passenger if she's comfortable.

"I just lost three people in my family," the passenger says.

"Oh, that's terrible," the flight attendant says, pausing for a moment. "No duty-free then?"

I expect the Colombo airport to be buzzing with activity. A massive recovery effort is supposedly under way. At Sri Lanka's main airport, however, there is little sign of it. No C-130s off-loading pallets of water and medicine, no line of trucks picking up supplies. A few Red Cross personnel wait for their colleagues to arrive, but there's no indication that a catastrophe has just occurred.

We drive south from Colombo, and the farther we go, the worse the scenes of destruction. There are few bulldozers, no heavy earth-moving equipment.

In every seaside town we drive through, villagers dig through rubble with their hands, or use crude tools to repair fishing boats splintered by the waves.

Thirty-five thousand people are dead in Sri Lanka. Their bodies have already been found. Another five thousand people have simply vanished.

CNN engineers have set up a satellite dish on the grounds of a destroyed beachfront hotel. Christmas decorations still hang from the lobby ceiling: SEASONS GREETINGS! HAPPY NEW YEAR!

Every morning near dawn for the next two weeks, we broadcast live from amid the hotel's rubble. Then Charlie Moore, my producer, and Phil Littleton, my cameraman, and I pile into a van and drive off, searching along the coast for stories. We end up working around the clock: shooting all day, writing and editing most of the night. Every report is the same: incalculable loss, unspeakable pain.

The single worst scene of carnage in Sri Lanka is just off the main road to Galle. When the tsunami hit, an old train packed with more than a thousand people was knocked off its tracks. At least nine hundred passengers died. For days they were unable to move the railcars and couldn't get to the bodies trapped in the smashed steel. When we arrive, however, most of the dead have finally been recovered. A few are still pinned underneath the train cars, submerged in ponds of seawater that have turned the ground to mud.

Two dogs brought in by Dutch volunteers search the wreckage. They are cadaver dogs and are specially trained to find dead bodies. The dogs are confused, however, there are so many scents; it's hard for them to stay focused.

"Everywhere we are searching, we find always bodies," one of the dog handlers tells me.

One of the demolished railcars came within a few feet of Dhanapala Kalupahana's house. He and his wife, Ariyawathie, are trying to clean up inside, but there is little they can do. Their roof has collapsed. It wasn't hit by the train; it fell under the weight of passengers who jumped onto it, trying to escape from the railcar. Several survived, but at least four people fell through the roof and died in Ariyawathie's living room, right in front of her eyes. She is barely able to speak. Her mother and son were also killed by the wave.

"Mother, no body. Son, no body" is all she can say.

Outside their home the jungle has become a gnarled mass of steel and mud, splintered trees, rotting flesh, and broken bones. I climb into a train car that was knocked off the tracks. Passengers' possessions are strewn about—a plate of food, a little girl's purse. Handprints smear the walls, a mixture of mud and blood. Everyone aboard drowned. Later I learn that the name of the train was Samudra Devi, the Goddess of the Sea.

At times, working in news is like playing a giant game of telephone. Someone reports something, and everyone else follows suit. The truth gets lost along the way.

"What about the kidnapped children?" a producer in New York asks.

"What kidnapped children?" I say.

"They claim lots of storm orphans are being kidnapped and sold into sexual slavery."

"Who's 'they'?" I ask.

"Everyone," the producer responds. "It's being reported all over the place."

"We'll look into it," I respond, which is usually the only way to end such a conversation.

Child trafficking is a major problem, especially in Southeast Asia, but when we start checking the kidnapping story being reported on other networks and papers, it seems slim on facts. It's mostly just aid workers worrying that children separated from their parents by the disaster may get kidnapped. Part of the aid workers' job is to get relief, and one way for them to do that is to raise red flags, warn of impending problems. Warnings, however, aren't facts.

We've hired a Sri Lankan newspaper reporter named Chris to help us get around, and when I ask him about kidnappings, his eyes light up. "Oh, yes, it appears a very big problem," he says, his British-accented English accompanied always with a peculiarly Sri Lankan shake of the head.

Chris shows us a headline on the front page of one of Sri Lanka's daily papers: TWO KIDS, RESCUED FROM WAVES, KIDNAPPED BY MAN ON MOTORCYCLE.

"There have been a lot of stories like that," he says. "It's all very dramatic stuff."

"Is it true?" I ask.

"I have no idea," he says, "but it makes for a great headline."

When we check with police, it turns out there have only been two complaints of child abductions filed with authorities, and neither of those cases has been confirmed. We decide to track down the story about the two kids kidnapped by the man on the motorcycle.

Sunera is seven, his sister Jinandari is five. They haven't been seen in nearly two weeks.

"I believe that they're alive," their aunt tells us when we track her down in Colombo. She speaks in a whisper and clutches a photograph of Jinandari dressed as a ballerina.

Sunera and Jinandari were in a car with their parents when the tsunami hit. The wave swept them off the road, carrying their car like a piece of driftwood some three hundred yards into a water-filled ditch. It ended up submerged upside down underwater, not far from the Lighthouse Hotel and Spa, a strikingly modern waterfront hotel near Galle.

When we arrive, the place is packed. It somehow survived the storm, and is now filled with reporters. They've converted the parking lot into a satellite-feed point. When we finally locate the manager, Ananda de Silva, he tells me, quite confidently, that the children are dead.

"From our staff, three people came and tried to turn the car," he tells me, pointing to the now dried-out ditch. "We couldn't do it, but after about thirty minutes, we were able to get the girl and boy out." The parents were dead, de Silva says, stuck in the car underwater. When they got Sunera out he was dead as well. Jinandari was unconscious.

"Her eyes were shut, her head like this," de Silva says, flopping his head forward.

"The paper says the children were kidnapped by a man on a motorcycle," I say, showing him the headline.

He waves his hand at the front page. "That is just rumor," de Silva says, insisting that he saw Sunera's body handed over to Sri Lankan soldiers passing by in a truck. As for Jinandari, he says that a man named Lal Hamasiri took her to the hospital on a motorbike.

Lal Hamasiri lives a short distance from the hotel. When we arrive, he is at first unwilling to speak, furious that local papers have made him out to be a kidnapper.

"I saw the child lying on the ground," he finally tells us, beckoning us into his home, away from the prying eyes of suspicious neighbors. "I imme-diately picked her up and gave her mouth to mouth. She had some white foam on her lips."

At the urging of the crowd, he flagged down a passing motorcycle and took the girl to a nearby hospital. "The body was a little warm, and I be-lieve she had a slight pulse," he says, but by the time they got to the emergency room, he was sure she was dead.

"I went up with the good intention of saving someone's life but in return I got a very bad name, and everyone looks at me like I'm a criminal, like I'm a kidnapper."

At the hospital, it quickly becomes obvious how a little girl can go missing. The emergency ward is washed away. Hospital beds sit abandoned in the courtyard, waterlogged papers and medical rec-ords litter the ground.

A short, squat man in a sparkling white suit waddles out of the main door, trailed by a fast-moving entourage; UN relief workers, Sri Lankan underlings, a few local news crews try to keep up with him.

"That's the fucking minister," our guide, Chris, tells me, pausing to watch the political parade pass by. According to him, this particular government minister was caught by his wife screwing another woman in his office. His wife created such a scene that the police were called, and the local tabloids had a feast.

"Oh, we went to town on that one," Chris says, his eyes wistful at the memory of it all. "Photos, eyewitness accounts, the whole nine yards."

When we finally track down the hospital administrator, she confirms that Jinandari was dead when she arrived. Because the morgue here had been demolished by the tsunami, they transferred her to another hospital. Even if she had been alive when she was pulled out of the water, the travel time alone to and from the hospitals would have killed her.

We decide that the least we can do is try to find Jinandari's body. Since we've come this far, it only seems right to see it through. When we reach the second hospital, we're directed down a long corridor and into a large, sun-filled room. It's the temporary morgue.

From outside, the room looks like an art gallery in New York's East Village. Hundreds of small photos line the walls. At first it's hard to tell what the photos show. You have to go up close, and even then it takes a moment for the images to snap into focus. They are pictures of the dead. More than a thousand of them. Every body that was stored here, every corpse, had its photograph taken, in the hopes that someone might be able to identify it.

No one ever talks about what the water can do. It's all here, however, color captured on film: the submersion, the struggle, the exhaustion, the fear. Water flooding into lungs, babies coughing and vomiting, hearts stopping, bodies convulsing, heads snapping back, startlingly white eyes popping from mud-smothered faces, tongues swelling into blackened balloons, necks bloating like those of giant toads, bones breaking, skulls crushing, teeth being ripped from heads, children from their mothers' arms.

In movies, people drown peacefully, giving in to the pull of the water, taken by the tug of the tide. These pictures tell a different story. There is no dignity in drowning, no silent succumbing to the water's ebb and flow. It's violent, and painful, a shock to the heart. Everyone drowns alone. Even in death, their corpses scream.

Nurses with face masks scrub the mottled floor with stiff brushes and brooms. Until a few days ago, the room was filled with bodies lying side by side on the floor. They've now been buried in a mass grave on the outskirts of town. It's the third time nurses are trying to disinfect the floor, but the rot and puss have seeped into the cement.

There are flies everywhere. Phil puts his camera down for a moment to change batteries. "Don't put that on the floor," the head nurse warns him, worried it might pick up bacteria. Hard as they've tried, they can't get the smell out. The stench of bodies is still there, buried under layers of bleach.

I've brought with me photos of Sunera and Jinandari—school portraits, the kind for which kids have to dress up, comb their hair, sit still. Each child smiles straight into the camera lens. I know Jinandari is somewhere on this wall of the dead, but staring at the pictures of the corpses, I know I'll never find her. The bodies are too decomposed.

"We should go," Charlie says, and I know he's right, but I keep forcing myself to look at the photos, stare at each face. I figure it's the least I can do.

Finally, we head out to find the mass grave, and reach it just as the sun is starting to set. There are no signs, just a swath of red clay stretching for hundreds of yards in a clearing in the woods. A bloodred slash in a forest of green, upturned earth as far as the eye can see.

Two women stand at the grave's edge. They live just behind it, in a small clearing.

"Why did they have to dig the graves here?" one of the women asks. "Now the ghosts of the dead will haunt us at night."

There are no headstones, no markers. The bodies are carried in by bulldozers and dumped into pits. New graves continue to be dug. No one knows for whom. The dead have no names. As we leave the burial ground and head back to the hotel, I check my watch. I notice the date. It's January 5, the day my father died.

———

I didn't know it was going to happen. I guess kids never do. I was ten. My father was fifty. That seemed old at the time; now its frighteningly young. My father died on an operating table at New York Hospital while undergoing heart bypass surgery. January 5, 1978. That was the date. I still mark it on my calendar every year. I should celebrate his birthday, of course, gather together friends who knew him, tell stories, keep his memory alive. Twenty-seven years later, it's still too painful even to try. Too raw. The nerves are still exposed. For years, I tried to swaddle the pain, encase the feelings. I boxed them up along with my father's papers, stored them away, promising one day to sort them all out. All I managed to do was deaden myself to them, detach myself from life. That works for only so long.

The morning my father went to the hospital, I was sick and stayed home from school. He came into my room and kissed me goodbye. He said he'd be back soon. He was hospitalized for nearly a month, and I got to visit him only once. They didn't allow children in the intensive care ward. I hated seeing him like that: lying in bed, an IV in his arm, a brown disinfectant stain on his hand. He seemed so weak, waiting for his heart to fail once again.

For Christmas he'd asked my mom to give my brother and me audio cassette recorders. I think he wanted me to tape my feelings, my fears. I never did. I wish now he'd recorded his voice, left me a message, one for each year he'd be gone. We planned to go to the hospital on Christmas Day, record our conversation. He had an attack that morning, however, and I never saw him alive again.

I was asleep when my mom came into my room to tell me he had died. I can't remember what she said, but I know she was crying. Soon my brother and I were as well.

She brought us into the living room. Al Hirschfeld, the cartoonist, was there with his wife, Dolly. They were close friends of my parents, and must have been with my mother at the hospital. I remember that Dolly told me about how she felt when her father died. From then on, every time I saw Hirschfeld's drawings in the Sunday **Times,** I thought about that night.

The day my father died, my life restarted. The person who I was disappeared, washed away by the turn of the tide. From time to time I still catch glimpses of the child I was when my father was alive: swimming through warm water in a crystal blue pool. Playing Marco Polo with my mom and dad. Dissolving into giggles as they get close. My hands reach out, touch their arms underwater. My legs wrap around my father's waist. My mother's hair is pulled back in a bun; my father smiles as I hold him tight. A seashell wind chime gently blows in the breeze. I can hear waves crashing somewhere through the hedges and over the dunes.

On a stretch of pale sand, a group of novice Sri Lankan monks in crimson tunics, children not yet teens, play with the outgoing tide. A thin boy in hand-me-down shorts and a mud-stained T-shirt watches from a distance. His name is Maduranga. He's thirteen years old, and his brother and sister were taken by the sea.

We're in a village called Kamburugamuwa. We found it quite by chance. There are no stores, no main street, just a cluster of simple homes and a mud path to the sea. Before the tsunami, visitors to the village were told to look for a Buddhist temple between the main road and the water. The temple is gone now; a slab of concrete, the building's foundation, is all that remains. There are children's schoolbooks and small colored plastic cups scattered about in the sand.

When the tsunami struck Kamburugamuwa, the temple was crowded. A Buddhist ceremony was taking place. Fifty-nine people had squeezed into the main room. Most sat facing the head monk, who was seated on a slightly raised dais, his back to the sea. Had there been a window behind the monk, perhaps some of those assembled would have seen the water coming, would have been able to escape. There was no window, however, no warning, no siren. There was chanting and incense, then water and death. Out of fifty-nine people in the temple that morning, only nine survived. Fifteen of the dead were children.

Phil Littleton, my cameraman, is South African. He's worked in Africa for much of his career and has developed both a strong dislike of authority and a wildly inappropriate sense of humor. I don't need to tell him what to do here. We all know why we've come.

"I'm going to go shoot around the temple," he tells me. "You know, 'the cups that the little hands will never touch again,' that sort of thing."

At first I'm shocked by his comment, but then I find myself laughing. He's making fun of us, of course, of what I'm thinking, of what Charlie is thinking as well. We've all seen the cups, all know what they represent; Phil has just spoken the words out loud. As a journalist, no matter how moved you feel, how respectful you are, part of your brain remains focused on how to capture the horror you see, how to package it, present it to others. We're here because children have died. Phil is just cutting to the chase. He's just getting what we came for.

Maduranga doesn't speak much English, but he shows me around what's left of his village, walking slowly through the labyrinth of huts and small houses made of cheap brick. He pauses by a muddy ditch and points to a spot about five feet away. "Sister," he says, and I realize that this is where his sister's body was found. A short distance away is his house, and next to it, in the backyard, is a mound of earth covered by a worn wooden board. It's his brother's grave. The wood is used to keep the rain off. Maduranga has no photos by which to remember his brother or his sister; soon even the mound will disappear. There will be no sign that either of them ever existed.

———————

My brother was twelve when my father died, and as hard as his death was for me, for my brother it must have been even worse. They'd had a more mature relationship. They'd shared a love of literature, and my brother often discussed with my father the history books he was reading. We were two years apart, but as kids, we were together all the time. A voracious reader of history and military campaigns, my brother had labeled me "Baby Napoleon" while I was still in my mom's womb, but he was the true leader of our childhood campaigns. He created giant battlefields for war games with our toy soldiers. The rules were too intricate for me to follow, but I loved to sit and watch him direct armies across the sweeping plains of our bedroom floor.

After the funeral, both of us retreated into separate parts of ourselves, and I don't think we ever truly reached out to each other again. I can't remember ever discussing my father's death with my brother. Perhaps I did, but I have no memory of it.

Suddenly the world seemed a very scary place, and I vowed not to let it get to me. I wanted to be autonomous, protect myself from further loss. I was only ten, but I decided I had to earn my own money, so I could save for a future I couldn't predict. I got a job as a child model and opened a bank account. My mother was wealthy, but I didn't want to have to rely on someone else.

In high school I started taking survival courses: month-long mountaineering expeditions in the Rockies, sea kayaking in Mexico. I needed to prove to myself that I could survive on my own. I left high school a semester early, and at seventeen I traveled for months by truck through southern and central Africa. I'd completed the credits I needed to graduate, and was sick of the pressure, wanted to forget about college and those silences at home filled by the murmur of television and the clanking of cutlery. Africa was a place to forget, and be forgotten in. My brother was already away at college. I assumed he'd come up with his own way to deal with the loss. I thought he could take care of himself.

He was smarter than me, more sensitive too. He lived much of his life in his head. In high school he fell in love with the writings of F. Scott Fitzgerald, with the fantasy of that lost world, and had gone to Princeton—I think in part because he hoped to discover that that way of life, Fitzgerald's world, was still alive. He was an idealist, impractical. He worried constantly about money, yet on impulse would buy a white double-breasted suit he saw in an ad. It hung in his closet unworn for years. I used to tease him about it—the waste of money, his lack of common sense.

I never thought of him as an older brother. It would have meant accepting that he was somehow looking out for me, that I wasn't independent, that I needed someone else.

Carter Vanderbilt Cooper. That was my brother's name. Strange. I rarely say it out loud anymore. I thought we had a silent agreement, that we would both just get through our childhoods and meet up as adults on the other side. I imagined one day we would be friends, allies, brothers laughing about our past fights. I'm not sure why he didn't keep his end of the bargain. Maybe he never knew about our silent pact. Maybe it was all in my head.

———

"Whenever we pass this temple my youngest points out and says, 'My brother died here,'" a mother in Kamburugamuwa tells me, her eyes watering. "I explain to him, 'Don't worry. He's in another world. He's in heaven now.'"

We've set up a camera in a classroom near the temple, and a half-dozen women sit outside, waiting for their chance to talk. Some clutch grainy photos of their lost children; some hold only their memories. Each wants to speak, however, wants her pain known, her child's absence felt.

"My daughter was very serious in her studies," one mother tells me. "My son; he was always messing around with the other kids." Both her children drowned in the temple. Their bodies were found near each other.

"I can't go home anymore," she says. "In my head, I see them messing around. I feel like my children are still playing out in the garden."

We will not be able to use all these women's words. It's too much detail, too many interviews to transcribe. So many mothers are waiting to talk, however. I can't turn any of them away.

"How do you go on?" I ask one mother.

She does not understand the question. "We have to go on," she finally says. "What choice do we have?"

"We all suffer together," another woman says, and for a moment I imagine she somehow knows my history, then am embarrassed that I would think that. She was with her six children at the temple when the wave hit. One of her daughters died. The rest survived by clinging to a coconut tree.

"It's better to talk," she says, "to tell stories to each other. It helps to overcome the grief."

What she says is true, I know that much, but I still find myself unable to do it, even though my pain isn't nearly as great. After my father died, my mother still talked about him, reminding us of things he'd said. I'd listen, nod my head, but I couldn't join in. I couldn't say a word. Walking in this village, listening to these people, is as close as I can come.

A fisherman named Dayratna stands in a grove behind his shack, hanging his daughter's wet schoolbooks in the branches of a tree. He wants to dry them out. The books are the only reminder he has of his daughter. Everything else—her photos, her clothes—were swept away. Dilini Sandarmali, that was her name. She was eleven years old.

"When I tried to remove my daughter's body from the temple," he whispers, his voice hoarse from crying, "I found her lying with two of her friends."

Dayratna is not sure what to do next. He won't return to work, because he can't face the sea. "I don't want to see the ocean again," he says wearily. "I curse the sea."

At first you want to know what happened in each house, to each heart, but after a while you no longer ask. Too much has already been said. The words fail to have meaning, fail to get at the depth of the sorrow. I look into the eyes of these mothers grieving for their children.

"I'm sorry for your loss," I say. It comes out sounding so small.

I find it hard to listen to these people's stories. They remind me so much of what I've lost, though compared with their suffering, mine seems minuscule. A minor misery, swallowed by the sea.

There was a time many years ago, when I first became a reporter, when I thought I could fake it. Go through the motions, not give away pieces of myself in return. I focused on the mechanics: storytelling and structure. I had conversations, conducted interviews, and I wasn't even there. I'd nod, look in others' eyes, but my vision lost focus, my mind turned to details. People became characters, plot lines in a story I was constructing in my head. Their mouths moved, I heard only lines of track, bites of sound. I listened for what I could use; the rest I fast-forwarded through.

When I had what I needed, I'd pull out. I thought I could get away unscathed, unchanged. The truth was I hadn't gotten out at all. It's impossible to block out what you see, what you hear. Even if you stop listening, the pain gets inside, seeps through the cracks you can't close up. You can't fake your way through it. I know that now. You have to absorb it all. You owe them that. You owe it to yourself as well.

"Sometimes you have to look very narrowly down the path," an aid worker in Somalia once said to me. "You can't look at what's lying on either side of the road."

I didn't understand what he meant at the time, but I certainly get it now. Crystal clear. If you are going to engage, then there's only so much you can stand. It's best not to stop in one place too long. A week or two, maximum. You can buy yourself more time if you have somewhere to stay away from the carnage. Then the story becomes a place you go to, venture from. It's an office, one that you prepare yourself for every morning.

In Sri Lanka, we sleep in a luxury hotel a few hours' drive away from the worst of the devastation. Each night we return to edit our footage and wolf down some dinner. A few tourists lounge in the last light of day: black-bikinied painted blondes with collagen lips, and Speedo-clad men with overhanging bellies and sunburned scalps. I see them laughing by the pool, sipping drinks with umbrellas, telling jokes in Russian and German. At first I'm shocked; I scream at them in my head, "Don't you know people have died here? How can you still lounge by the pool?" But I say nothing, of course. Why shouldn't they lounge? Elsewhere in the world life continues. That's just how it is.

When we leave Kamburugamuwa, I notice that we're quiet. Even Phil has been silenced by the sadness of it all. A truck filled with Buddhist monks chanting through a loudspeaker passes us by. Their deep-throated droning wafts over what remains of the small village. Maduranga is standing by the water's edge. Alone on the beach. A sad little boy. He throws stones at the sea.

In April 1988, my brother showed up at my mother's apartment and said he wanted to move back home. She lived in a duplex on New York's Upper East Side. It was a penthouse we'd moved into when my brother and I were in high school. The building faced the East River, and each floor had a wrap-around terrace, which gave anyone in the apartment the feeling of being on a ship. Driving along the river, you could see the balcony off my room silhouetted against the skyline. Whenever I was approaching the place in a taxi on the FDR Drive, I'd count to see how many seconds it took me to see the ledge.

My brother was living in his own apartment in the city. He was an editor for **American Heritage,** a history magazine, and also wrote book reviews for **Commentary.** He'd recently broken up with his girlfriend. They'd met in college and had dated for several years, but I wasn't aware how serious it was. The truth is, I didn't pay much attention. When they broke up, we talked about it on the phone, but not in any great detail. I'd never broken up with someone I was in love with, and I didn't appreciate the pain of such a loss.

That day in April, when Carter told our mom he wanted to move back home, he came to a race of mine. I was a junior at Yale, a coxswain on the lightweight crew, and the team was in New York competing against Columbia University. Carter had never been to a race of mine before, and I was excited that he was coming. When he arrived, however, he seemed disheveled, distracted. I knew instantly that something was wrong. He watched my race, but left soon after. When I stopped home, my mom told me that he was upset about something and had taken several days off work. She'd gotten him a recommendation for a therapist, and Carter had agreed to start seeing him.

I slipped into the guest room where he was sleeping—his old bedroom was being used largely for storage—and sat on the edge of his bed. That night, he seemed scared, fragile, and that frightened me, made me angry. I resented his weakness. I asked him how he was, and we talked about his job a bit, but I really didn't want to know too much. It sickens me now to realize all this, to see how selfish I was. I could have done something that might have helped. I could have talked to him, opened up, let him know that he wasn't alone. But I didn't. I left for school early the next morning.

A few days afterward, my mom told me that Carter liked the therapist and had returned to work. He'd also decided not to move back home. I was relieved, eager for any reason to stop worrying about him, to pretend that his crisis had never happened. I assumed that whatever problems he was having he'd confide to his therapist. I later learned he did not.

———————

In every tragedy, people search for miracles, signs that sustain them even when surrounded by death. We've been in Sri Lanka for more than a week when Chris, our interpreter, tells us about a small church in the town of Matera.

"Very strange comings and goings," he says, clearly excited. "Levitating statues, miracles even."

The church is named after a five-hundred-year-old relic, Our Lady of Matera, a finely carved figure of the Virgin Mary and the baby Jesus that has stood in an alcove near the altar for as long as anyone can remember.

When the first wave struck, Father Charles Hewawasam was at the altar, preparing communion for some one hundred parishioners seated on simple wooden benches inside. The choir in the balcony had just begun to sing the first few lines of a hymn, "While Shepards Watched."

Father Charles didn't see the wave. He remembers hearing a crash, which he thought was a traffic accident on a nearby street. Seconds later, he was swimming in water. There were screams, and bodies, cars floating in the nave, chunks of stone and wood. Everything smelled of the sea.

"I remember three bodies floating near the altar," Father Charles tells me when we arrive at the church. He is in his early thirties with black hair combed neatly and parted on one side. He still limps slightly from an injury to his leg, and he speaks soft British-accented English, looking you straight in the eye when he talks.

Father Charles introduces us to a nine-year-old boy named Dimaker, who was standing in the balcony when the water swept over the congregation beneath him. Dimaker sang in the choir, and was still holding his hymnal when he says he saw the statue of Our Lady of Matera rise from its pedestal in the alcove and leave the church.

"She was not taken by the water," Dimaker explains, motioning with his hands to show how the statue seemed to levitate. "She went on her own. It was a miracle."

Twenty people died in the church that morning. Some were killed by the initial impact; others drowned trying to escape. Father Charles didn't notice that the statue was gone until later that day, when Dimaker told him what he'd seen.

"I believe she went out to sea to be with the people, her children," Father Charles tells me. "She went with the people and she carried Jesus. She had the same struggle as the other people."

For three mornings after the tsunami, Father Charles tells me, he went to the ocean's edge and prayed for the return of the statue. "We need you," he'd say out loud. "You have to come back."

Each day, he attended to the burials of his parishioners and looked after the needs of the wounded. Several people from his congregation were missing, and parts of the church had been badly damaged. Father Charles believed he couldn't complete his mission without Our Lady by his side.

"We've much work to do," he said on the second morning after the tsunami, as he stood praying on the shore. "You have to come back."

At night in his simple room on church grounds, he prayed for the people of Matera, but each morning he'd return to the beach.

It was on the third day after the tsunami that Father Charles says his prayers were answered. That morning, as he stood on the shore, he implored the statue to return.

"My goodness, you have to come today," he said. "You can't wait anymore."

A few hours later a child came to the church and spoke with one of the deacons. He'd found something lying in bushes about a mile from the shrine. It was the statue, intact. Even the delicate gold crown on baby Jesus's head had remained in place.

When Father Charles was summoned, he could barely contain himself, so sure was he that it was the work of God.

Nearly two weeks later, when I talk with him, we stand on the beach in the spot where he prayed each morning. His white cassock flutters in the breeze, and he clutches a black rosary in his hand. He is more convinced than ever that God has watched over Matera.

"Lives are lost, and we are still looking for so

many people," he says. "For the statue to come back, it's a miracle. I think these people who've died have sacrificed for a better cause. Our country was divided politically and along ethnic lines, and now we don't think about divisions. When I do the burials, when I visit the mortuaries, and I see all the bodies together, just the same, without any clothes, it shows whatever the faith, whatever the culture, the color, we are all human in the end."

The statue of Our Lady of Matera was taken to the bishop's office, where it will be stored until the church is repaired. The day the statue is returned, Father Charles and his parishioners intend to walk through the streets of Matera with it. A procession of survivors, showing Our Lady that their faith is still alive.

You always hear stories about brothers who sense each other's pain. Brothers so close that when one is in danger, the other knows it, feels it. This isn't one of those stories. The night my brother died, I was hundreds of miles away, in Washington, sitting on a subway. At the moment it happened, I didn't feel a thing.

I'd only seen him once since April, when he'd appeared at my crew race scared and disoriented. We'd talked on the phone, but never for very long. The day I saw him, I was interning in Washington, but had come to New York for a long weekend. By chance I ran into him on the street. It was the day before the Fourth of July.

"The last time I saw you, I was like an animal," he said. I wasn't sure what he meant, and I didn't know what to say, but I took it as a good sign that he was joking about our last encounter. We went for a hamburger, and parted soon after. I can't remember if we hugged or not. He said he'd see me later that weekend. He didn't. I never saw him alive again.

———————

On July 22, 1988, my brother showed up at my mother's apartment early in the morning, unexpectedly. It was a Friday, and once again he said that he wanted to move back in. He seemed out of sorts, nervous, and said he hadn't slept the night before. Throughout the day, he took several naps in my old bedroom, on the second floor of the duplex. When she checked on him, my mother noticed he'd opened the sliding glass door to the balcony. It was a summer day, and the heat was overwhelming.

"Don't you want me to turn on the air conditioner?" she asked him.

"No," he said. "It's fine the way it is."

They ate lunch together, and talked. My mother was concerned, but not overly so. She knew that something was wrong, but Carter wouldn't say what. After lunch she let him sleep for a time, then checked on him to see if there was anything he wanted. At some point, as he lay on the sofa in the library, she read him a story by Michael Cunningham called "White Angel," which had just been published in **The New Yorker.** In the story, a young boy unexpectedly dies after he runs through a plate-glass sliding door in his parents' living room while they are having a party. A shard of glass severs an artery in his neck. The violence of the story surprised my mom, but it didn't seem to upset Carter.

"That was a good story," he said.

He took another nap.

At about 7:00 P.M., he came into my mom's room. He appeared dazed, disoriented.

"What's going on? What's going on?" he asked.

"Nothing's going on," my mother said soothingly.

"No, no," he said shaking his head. He ran from her room, "as if he knew where he was going, knew the destination," she would later tell me. My mother followed him as he ran up the curving staircase, into my room, through the sliding glass door, and onto the balcony.

By the time she got there, he was perched on the low stone wall that surrounded the terrace outside my room. His right foot was on top of the wall, his left foot was touching the terrace floor.

"What are you doing?" she cried out, and started moving toward him.

"No, no. Don't come near me," he said.

"Don't do this to me, don't do this to Anderson, don't do this to Daddy," my mother pleaded.

"Will I ever feel again?" he asked.

My mother is not sure how long they were out there on the terrace. It all happened very fast. He looked down at the ground, fourteen stories below. A helicopter passed overhead, a glint of silver in the late-summer sky. Then he moved.

"He was like a gymnast," my mother remembers. "He went over the ledge and hung on the edge like it was a practice bar in a gym."

"I shouted, 'Carter, come back!'" she told me later, "just for a moment I thought he was going to. But he didn't. He just let go."

In ancient Rome, priests called haruspices, charged with predicting the future, would push their hands deep into the innards of freshly killed animals. They removed the heart, the liver, the entrails, and splayed them out on an altar to divine the will of the Gods. I see no signs in Sri Lanka's bloodied remains, no augury of what 2005 will hold. I'm searching for stories about what has already happened. I've missed the warnings about what lies ahead, the signs of what's to come.

After two weeks in Sri Lanka, I return to New York. I thought I'd dream of that train wreck, of Sunera and Jinandari, Maduranga, Father Charles, and all the others whose gazes I held and hands I touched. I don't. Instead, I dream of the ocean, and all those still trapped deep beneath. Their eyes open, their hair swaying with the tide. Thousands of people submerged in silence, preserved in the cold saltwater, entombed. Thousands of people. Together. Alone.

It took several hours for my mother to find me after my brother's suicide. By the time I got her call, the last shuttle had already left Washington, so I rented a car at the airport and drove through the night.

I can't remember what she said to me on the phone, the actual words she used. I just recall the shock in her voice. I could picture the stunned look in her eyes. I didn't want to talk to anyone, didn't want to be consoled. Since my father's death, I'd wanted to control my life, control access to my emotions. When I heard that my brother was dead, I dove deeper into myself. I retreated, hoping to block the shock, the reeling fear, the wave of nausea that made me clutch my stomach.

I was sad, of course, but I was angry as well. How could he have done this to our mother, killed himself in front of her? How could he have left me behind to deal with the mess?

It was dawn when I reached New York. On the FDR Drive I searched the skyline for my mother's apartment building. Out of habit I counted, seeing how long it would take me to find my balcony. Five seconds. When I spotted it I realized that it was the ledge my brother had jumped from. I wondered if someone driving on this road had seen him do it. He would have appeared as just a small speck hurtling through the air, disappearing into the sidewalk below.

In the four days between my brother's death and his funeral, it seemed as if we were marooned on an ice floe broken off from a glacier. We didn't leave the apartment. A giant chasm had opened up around us, and we were suddenly separate from the rest of the world.

My mother lay in bed retelling the story of Carter's death to each person who came to visit her, as if by repeating it she'd discover some new piece of information that would explain it all, would perhaps reveal that it hadn't really happened, that it was all a misunderstanding, a terrible dream.

"Like a gymnast," she'd say to each new visitor. I knew it helped her to go over and over it, combing the sand for some clue, some shard that would bring Carter back. No matter how many times I heard the story, however, it still didn't make any sense.

After a while I stopped listening. The story didn't get me any closer to understanding. If anything, it pointed out what wasn't known, and what might never be. "Why?" That's the question everyone asked: Why kill himself? Why do it in front of his mother? Why didn't he leave a note?

Sometimes my mother wept, and screamed. I think I envied her that. I cried, but at night, in my pillow, not wanting others to hear. I suppose I worried that if I let go, I, too, would fall off the edge, plunge into whatever blackness had swept my brother away.

A handful of reporters and cameramen waited outside the building. It didn't occur to me that this had become a media event until my mother's lawyer accidentally left a copy of the **New York Post** in the apartment. HEIR'S TRAGIC LAST HOURS was the headline on the front page. They kept referring to my mother as the "Poor Little Rich Girl," a tag that tabloids had given her as a child at the height of her mother and aunt's custody battle. I threw the paper out. I didn't want my mother to see that she was once again in the headlines.

When we arrived at the Frank E. Campbell Funeral Chapel for Carter's wake, about a half-dozen photographers snapped pictures as I helped my mom out of the car. I hated them: circling like vultures over our barely breathing bodies.

I'd forgotten that moment, that feeling, until this past year, when I found myself reporting outside Terri Schiavo's hospice watching a jostling crowd of cameramen follow her father's and mother's every move. Schiavo was in a persistent vegetative state, and her feeding tube had been removed. Her parents were fighting to have it put back in.

"Khraw, khraw," a producer standing next to me screeched, mimicking the sound of circling buzzards.

"I've become what I once hated," I thought to myself—sadly, not for the first time.

Carter's casket was in the largest room the funeral home had, but the line of mourners stretched down the block. My mom stood receiving people, one by one looking into their eyes for answers.

There had been no invitations issued, so it wasn't possible to control who got on the line. I ended up screening those gathered, pulling some close friends off the queue and telling them just to come in. Occasionally I'd approach a stranger, trying to find out who he or she was. Several were merely curious passersby. One man was holding a copy of the **New York Post** and wanted my mom to autograph it. I thanked him for coming and asked someone to show him out.

My brother was wearing a gray Paul Stuart suit. I'd gone to his apartment the day before the wake to pick it out. When I'd seen the suit in his closet, I'd wanted it for myself, then felt guilty for being selfish, so I decided that that was the suit he should be buried in. In the taxi on my way home, I sat with it on my lap. The radio was on, and an interviewer was saying to a caller, "Hey, I mean look at that Vanderbilt kid. I mean the interest on his trust fund was probably more than I'll make in my lifetime, and that didn't stop him from jumping off a building. I mean, am I right or what?"

The morticians had parted my brother's hair on the wrong side. "Oh, no, that's not him," I almost said. "There's been some kind of mistake."

I noticed a silver screw with a bolt sticking out of the back of his head. I hoped my mom couldn't see it. If she did, she showed no sign. Before we left, we stood together by the casket. My mother looked at my brother's face, and closed her eyes for a moment. Then, just as she had with my father, she asked for a pair of scissors, and cut off a lock of Carter's hair.

———————

My final year of college was a blur. I spent most of my time trying to understand what had happened, worried that whatever dark impulse had driven my brother to his death might still be lurking somewhere out there, waiting for me.

Many times that year, I wished I had a mark, a scar, a missing limb, something children could have pointed at, at which adults could tell them not to stare. At least then they would have seen, would have known. I wouldn't have been expected to smile and mingle, meet and greet. Everyone could have seen that, like a broken locket, I had only half a heart.

Senior year became a series of holidays and celebrations to avoid. My mother and I ordered Chinese takeout on Thanksgiving, watched movies on Christmas. We stopped giving gifts, ignored each other's birthdays. Each event was a reminder of what we'd lost. On weekends I'd take the train back to New York. We'd eat dinner at home, mostly stay indoors. For the first few months, I slept in the guest room downstairs, unable to set foot in my own room or look at the balcony outside it. My mother talked about Carter, went over theories in her head. I listened but couldn't add much. It was like staring into a bottomless chasm. I worried that there was nothing to stop me from falling if I took the next step. I was there, I listened, we were together. It was all I was capable of.

I graduated college nearly a year after my brother died. My mom came up to New Haven, we took some pictures, and that was it. She returned to New York to pack up the apartment and move to a townhouse on the other side of the city. She no longer wanted to live in a penthouse. After my brother's death, both of us developed a fear of heights. I asked her what she thought I should do for work, now that I'd graduated.

"Follow your bliss," she said, quoting Joseph Campbell. I was hoping for something more specific—"Plastics," for instance. I worried I couldn't "follow my bliss" because I couldn't feel my bliss; I couldn't feel anything at all. I wanted to be someplace where emotions were palpable, where the pain outside matched the pain I was feeling inside. I needed balance, equilibrium, or as close to it as I could get. I also wanted to survive, and I thought I could learn from others who had. War seemed like my only option.

Iraq
INKBLOTS OF BLOOD

In college I'd read a lot about the Vietnam War and the foreign correspondents who covered it. Their tales of night patrols and hot LZs made reporting sound like an adventure, one that was also worthwhile. News, however, is a hard business to break into. After college, I applied for an entry-level job at **ABC News**—photocopying, answering phones—but after months of waiting, I couldn't even get an interview. Such is the value of a Yale education.

I finally got a job as a fact-checker at **Channel One,** a twelve-minute daily news program broadcast to thousands of high schools throughout the United States. I knew that fact-checking wasn't going to get me anywhere close to a front line, but I needed to get my foot in the door somehow. After several months of working there, I came up with a plan to become a foreign correspondent. It was very simple, and monumentally stupid.

I figured if I went places that were dangerous or exotic, I wouldn't have much competition, and if my stories were interesting and inexpensive, **Channel One** might broadcast them. A colleague of mine agreed to make a fake press pass for me on a Macintosh computer, and loan me one of his Hi-8 cameras. I didn't really know what I was doing, but I'd watched a lot of TV news growing up, and had some idea how stories were put together. The rest I figured I'd learn along the way.

I quit my job as a fact-checker, but didn't inform the producers who ran **Channel One** of my plan. I figured they'd tell me not to go, or refuse to look at whatever material I shot. In December 1991, I flew to Thailand and met up with some Burmese refugees who were working to overthrow their country's military dictatorship. Apparently, my fake press pass was convincing because they agreed to sneak me across the Thai-Burmese border so I could shoot a story about their struggle.

Their camp was in dense jungle. Throughout the day, you could hear mortar fire in the distance from an unseen front line. I found it all very exciting, and loved being in a position to ask questions and shoot pictures. None of it seemed very real to me, however, until I went to the field hospital where young soldiers, many just teenagers, lay with bloody wounds and missing limbs.

A doctor in surgical scrubs was operating on the leg of a young man whose face was badly bruised; his eyes had turned milky white. I saw the doctor reach for a stainless-steel saw, and at first didn't understand what he was going to do with it. When he began cutting the teenager's leg off, I nearly passed out. The soldiers who were escorting me laughed.

Channel One bought the video I'd shot, and when I arrived back in Bangkok, I knew that this was the career I wanted. I couldn't imagine doing anything else. I called my mom and told her, "I think I've found my bliss."

Shortly after I get back from Sri Lanka in the middle of January 2005, I notice that, professionally, something has changed. TV reporters call me requesting interviews about the tsunami. Colleagues tell me what a good job I've done. I appreciate the compliments, and don't want to seem ungrateful, but the praise makes me uncomfortable. I'm glad people are interested in the story, but when they ask me what it was like, I'm not sure what to say. I don't know how to sum it up in a sound bite. I don't know what to do with the sudden spotlight. It's easier just to go back overseas, so I volunteer to go to Iraq.

Elections for a new interim government are scheduled to take place at the end of January. They'll be the first real elections Iraq's had since Saddam.

This is my second trip to Iraq for CNN, and I'm still not sure what I've really seen. "Everyone has a different war," a soldier once said to me. "We all see our own little slice; no one ever sees it the same." Roger that.

Iraq is a Rorschach test. You can see what you want in the inkblots of blood. Number of attacks is down, lethality is up. Kidnappings fall, IEDs rise. More Iraqis are trained, more police desert. Fewer Americans die, more Iraqi cops get killed. One step forward, a bomb blast back. So many words written, so many pundits positioned. The closer you look, the harder it is to focus.

On the morning flight from Amman, Jordan, to Baghdad you see all kinds: the desperate, the downtrodden, the curious, the convinced, true believers, truth seekers, patriots, and parasites. In Iraq they hope to find money or meaning, or something in between. The plane is Jordanian, the pilots and flight attendants South African. In Iraq, they know there's money to be made.

War is hell, but hell, it's also an opportunity.

The flight proceeds normally, until the last few minutes. Rather than making a long slow descent to the runway, the plane banks sharply, turning in a corkscrew motion directly over the Baghdad airport.

"The final part of our descent will be from overhead the airfield in a spiral fashion," the pilot announces. "It may feel a little uncomfortable on the body but it's a perfectly safe maneuver."

Of course, if it were perfectly safe they wouldn't be doing the maneuver, but it's the best protection they have against getting shot out of the sky by a rocket-propelled grenade.

WELCOME TO FREE IRAQ. That's what it says on the T-shirts they sell at Baghdad International Airport. Freedom's great, but so is security, and right now most Iraqis would trade a lot of the first for even some of the second.

In the Arrivals terminal, a Filipino clutching a machine gun shouts instructions to a gaggle of Halliburton employees who've just arrived. Printed on the back of the Filipino's baseball cap is the name of the security company he works for: CUSTER BATTLES. It doesn't exactly inspire confidence.

Every reporter likes to believe that what they're seeing and feeling is unique, that it hasn't already been seen and felt a thousand times in other places, other conflicts. I try to keep the stories separate, not allow what I've seen in one country to change how I see things someplace else. It's not always easy. I set up barriers in my head, my heart, but blood flows right through them. A corpse I see in Baghdad will remind me of a body back in Bosnia. Sometimes I can't even remember where I was or why. I just remember the moment, the look, a sudden snap of a synapse, a blink of an eye, and I'm in another conflict, another year. Every war is different, every war the same.

———————

Sarajevo. March 1993. Bosnia wasn't my first war, but at the time, it was the deadliest one I'd seen. It had taken me nearly a year after Burma, but **Channel One** had finally hired me as a correspondent. I was twenty-five, still shooting my stories on a home video camera, and traveling all alone, but at least now they were picking up the bills.

It was the first year of the war in Bosnia, and Sarajevo was under siege. Serbs in surrounding mountains lobbed shells into the city, mortaring the marketplace where old men sold their broken watches and tried to hold onto their dignity. A shell would land, blood splattered the street. You could feel the impact blocks away. There were snipers as well. Their bullets cut through the air, silent, spinning. No tracer fire, no warning. Just snap, crackle, pop, and a body would crumple to the ground.

Anyone who tells you they aren't scared in a war zone is a fool or a liar, and probably both. The more places you've been, the more you know just how easy it is to get killed. It's not like in the movies. There are no slow-motion falls, no crying out the names of your loved ones. People die, and the world keeps spinning.

I flew into Sarajevo from Zagreb, Croatia, on a UN charter. **Channel One** had just given me a brand-new flak jacket, but I hadn't bothered to take it out of its plastic wrapping until the plane was just about to land. When I did, I noticed something sewn inside. It was a warning label: THIS VEST DOES NOT PROTECT AGAINST ARMOR-PIERCING PRO-

JECTILES, RIFLE FIRE, SHARP OR POINTED INSTRU-
MENTS.

It was useless against snipers, effective only against pistols, close-range stuff. In Sarajevo, they killed you from far away.

I put the vest on anyway and walked alone into the sandbag maze of Sarajevo's airport. On the flight, there had been only one other passenger: a young German kid with a camera. He looked more scared than I did, and seemed to have even less of a clue about what he was getting himself into. He never even left the airport. I heard he flew back to Zagreb that same day.

I was afraid to sleep in the bed in my room at the Holiday Inn. I kept thinking some shrapnel might kill me during the night. So I'd lay on the floor, trying to sleep, listening to the dull thud of mortars landing on nearby buildings. Like a mangy dog, the Holiday Inn had sunk its teeth into Sarajevo, and wasn't letting go. Most of the glass in the hotel was already cracked or broken. It had been replaced with heavy plastic sheeting. During the winter, the wind whipped and whistled down the darkened corridors.

Everyone still called it the Holiday Inn, though I heard that the chain had revoked its franchise. Given the constraints imposed by the Serbian stranglehold on Sarajevo, the hotel just couldn't maintain the high standards demanded by the parent corporation. The bed mints had run out a long time ago.

During the 1984 Winter Olympics, the location of the hotel was ideal; it was in the heart of the city, near the river, with views of the mountains. During the war, however, the location couldn't have been worse. The ski slopes that once hosted competitors from around the world were now home to snipers. The boxy Holiday Inn was a top-heavy target. It faced the front line, and at night, tracer fire whipped past the windows like shooting stars.

Channel One hadn't bothered to rent me an armored vehicle, but they did get me a two-door Yugo. Not exactly an equal substitute, but it was better than nothing. I hired a local reporter named Vlado to show me around. He kept calling the Yugo a "soft-skin" car, which didn't exactly fill me with confidence. The morning after I arrived, I came downstairs to find that someone had stolen the car's windshield wipers. Just the wiper blades. They left the sticks that held them. They were bent forward, jutting out from the base of the windshield. As we drove, they rotated like spinning horns. It made us laugh at first, but after awhile there was something sad about them. The next day, Vlado ripped them off entirely.

The front entrance to the hotel was boarded up, and to get in you had to go through a side door. Vlado would drive us around the back of the hotel, trying to keep the car protected from snipers for as long as possible. Just before he reached the side entrance, he'd have to jump a curb, and every time he did, I was sure the tires would blow out.

The day before I left, I was out on my own, a few blocks from the hotel. I thought I was in a protected spot. I was planning on doing what TV reporters call a "stand-up"—in which they talk to the camera—and I'd just set up my tripod when I heard a loud crack. I turned and saw a tile fall off a nearby column. By the time it hit the ground, I realized that it had been struck by a bullet. Someone had taken a shot. I didn't know if they were shooting at me or someone else, but it didn't matter. I ran behind a nearby building, and the sniper peppered the area with automatic fire. I captured some of it on camera, and narrated what I was seeing. I was white as a corpse. When I looked at the tape recently, though, I saw something I hadn't remembered. I noticed the faint hint of a smile on my face.

Sometimes the places that are the most dangerous don't feel that bad at all. In Baghdad there are moments when you think nothing can touch you. Encased in Kevlar, puffed up like some B-movie cyborg, you peer through double-paned bullet-proof glass at the dust and decay, the cement blast barriers. You watch people on the street and wonder who's good, who's bad, who'll live, who'll die. You're surrounded by guys with barrel chests and ceramic plates hidden underneath their shirts, machine guns ready, safeties unlocked. Who knows what else they have in their bags?

You're trapped in a bubble of security; you can't break out—with guards and guns, and no time to linger on the street, it's hard to tell what's really going on. Bulletproof glass protects but it also distorts. Fear alters everything.

It's late January 2005, and I've come to Iraq to cover the interim elections for CNN. We're driving in from Baghdad's airport, on a road the army calls Route Irish.

"They say this is the most dangerous road in the world," my driver says.

"They always do," I say, and I realize I sound like a jerk.

Every war has a road like this one, the most dangerous, the most mined. I don't know how you can judge.

Baghdad's Route Irish connects the airport to the Green Zone. It's an eight-mile haul but there's a two-mile stretch that's particularly bad. Snipers, improvised explosive devices, ambushes, suicide attacks—you name it, it's happened on Route Irish. U.S. soldiers patrol the road and the surrounding neighborhoods, but the attacks keep happening.

After **Wall Street Journal** reporter Daniel Pearl was kidnapped and murdered in Pakistan in 2002, news companies began to take security much more seriously. In Baghdad most major American news organizations contract with private security firms. Big guys with thick necks meet you at the airport and give you a bulletproof vest before they even shake your hand.

The company that CNN contracts with provides former British Special Forces soldiers—tough professional men who've done things you can't imagine, in places you've never heard of. They don't talk much about where they've been, but they'll tell you right away: Baghdad's the worst they've seen.

The city is crawling with security **contractors,** a ghost army of more than 10,000 private guards. In other times, other places, they'd be called mercenaries, but here **contractors** is the preferred term.

"Look at that GI Joe," one of my guards says, pointing to a contractor manning a roadblock. "Isn't he all decked out."

You see all kinds: from former Navy SEALS who know what they're doing, and keep a low profile, to weekend warriors you don't want to get anywhere near. The latter swagger around the city tricked out in ninja gear: commando vests, kneepads, pistols on hips, knives in boots, machine guns at the ready. A little overweight, a lot down on their luck, for them Iraq came along at just the right time. A year here, and they can earn two hundred thousand dollars. The ones who worry me the most are South Africans—Afrikaners: big buzz-cut blonds with legs like tree trunks. They come for the money and the frontier freedom. One of my security guards complains that they're out of control.

"I saw some South Africans shoot up the grill of

a car that was driving behind them," he tells me, shaking his head. "There was no reason, they did it just because they could."

There's not a lot of talking in the car on the way from the airport. I want to shoot a story about driving on Route Irish, and planned to videotape my guards, and the drama of the ride into Baghdad, but when I take out my camera, they strongly suggest that I put it away. They don't want anyone knowing who they are.

Even in an armored car, we have to wear Kevlar vests. If we got ambushed, insurgents might be able to disable the car, then we'd have to take our chances outside. That's when the vest could come in handy. The guards radio our location constantly to CNN's office so that if we're kidnapped, CNN will at least know where it happened.

Thousands of Iraqis use Route Irish each day. The traffic moves in fits and starts; cars merge from unseen on-ramps. That's often from where attacks are launched.

We drive fast, constantly scanning the traffic around us. A car suddenly appears out of nowhere. It's coming up quickly behind us. Eyes dart. Bodies shift.

"Four guys, young, bearded," one of my guards says into a walkie-talkie.

"Ali Babas," says another, using the universal term for bad guys.

We stay tense, expect an attack, but nothing happens. The car swerves off; another takes its place. After awhile I stop paying attention, stop noticing my heart pounding against the Kevlar.

"This road, I think it's the most dangerous in world, you know?" my driver said, smiling.

"Yes, I know," I said. "Thanks for reminding me."

This was on another trip to Sarajevo. I think it was 1994, into the war's second year. I had an armored Land Rover this time. The airport was shut down—too many mortars, too many snipers. The only road in and out of Sarajevo zigzagged down Mount Igman, a small dirt-and-gravel lane with hairpin turns. It scared me more than I liked to admit. Every now and then we'd pass the rusted remains of shot-up trucks, which only added to the **Apocalypse Now** feel of the trip.

At first I kept quizzing the driver at every turn: "This stretch, coming up, is this dangerous?"

He'd just smile. After a while, I stopped asking. It was all so dangerous; there was no point talking about it. You just had to sit back and hope the morning mist held long enough to cover you, or hope the Serb snipers were too hungover to aim straight. Luck, fate, God—you believed in whatever got you down the mountain. I put my faith in the Clash, and made a couple promises to God just in case. (I like to cover all my bases.) My driver seemed crazy, perhaps manic-depressive, but in Sarajevo that wasn't unusual. He was a big, bald, good-looking Bosnian, who attempted to screw just about every woman we came in contact with. He seemed to succeed more often than not. I'd get into the armored Land Rover in the morning, and there'd be a used condom on my seat.

"Jesus Christ, do you have to have sex in the car?" was usually how I greeted him.

"I know," he'd say, "but what can I do? It's the safest place to fuck."

It was hard to argue with his logic. In another place I would have been annoyed at having to work with him, but in Sarajevo, especially on the Mount Igman road, he was exactly the kind of guy I wanted behind the wheel. He always drove fast, but when the road got bad, he'd floor it. Sometimes he'd curse the Serbs, call their mothers jackals and their daughters whores. That's when I knew we were on a particularly bad stretch. When he began to spit, I'd buckle up.

The last time I came down the Mount Igman road, I caught a glimpse of myself in the side-view mirror. "Charlie Don't Surf" was blaring from the cassette player and my face was completely drained of color; my eyebrows were furrowed, my mouth frozen in a lunatic grin. When we finally made it into the city, I was so relieved, all I could do was laugh. The driver looked at me as if I were the one who was crazy. Then he started laughing too.

———————

From the headlines and pictures you'd think Iraq was complete chaos, but the truth is much more complicated. I learned this during my first trip here for CNN. It was June 2004, and I'd come to cover the handover of power from the Coalition Provisional Authority to an interim Iraqi government. I went on patrol with the U.S. First Cavalry in charge of Route Irish. A routine recon—buttoned-down Bradleys, up-armored Humvees.

"It's nowhere near as bad as you see on TV," a

young soldier said to me. "Sure, you get shot at sometimes, but mostly it's real boring."

On TV they fast-forward to the most dramatic images; they rarely mention the downtime. On patrol it's the opposite: the hours tick by slowly; it's easy to become complacent. It was 110 degrees, and the young reservists were drenched in sweat, their skin wet under camouflage vests and behind wraparound glasses. In Baghdad you can't see anyone's eyes.

"I'm sweating more than an E-six trying to read," Ryan Peterson joked, poking fun at his staff sergeant, his hands never far from the machine gun mounted on the back of the Humvee. Peterson had been on a patrol that was ambushed two months before, and he knew damn well there was nothing he could do to stop it from happening again. The truck's armor plating reached only up to Peterson's waist, so standing in the back together, we were partially exposed. We didn't have much choice.

"What do you think about Iraq?" I asked him.

"This place?" he said, shrugging and looking around as if he'd just noticed it for the first time. "Could go either way at this point, either way."

I didn't bother asking him if he cared.

"When the bullets start flying," Master Sergeant

James Ross told me, "all that 'Huah,' 'Army of One' stuff goes out the window. All you care about is the soldiers around you, that's it." Ross should know: during the ambush he had had to run across an open field under fire. Now he's convinced he'll get out of here alive.

"I don't know why," he told me quietly, "but I just got this feeling."

That day, the patrol was looking for IEDs and delivering water to a neighborhood near Route Irish. The kind of mission they went on every day.

"Is this part of the plan to 'win hearts and minds'?" I asked one of the officers.

He laughed. "We're not trying to win any hearts and minds," he said, making fun of the phrase as he spoke it. "That dog ain't gonna hunt. Right now we're just trying to co-opt as many of them as we can. At this point, that's about all we can do."

The army was giving money away to local leaders, creating construction projects to keep men working. They handed out comic books for kids, and for adults, cigarettes with toll-free numbers printed on the packs, so they could easily inform on their neighbors.

After ten hours, the patrol ended. The soldiers cleared their weapons as they pulled into their heavily fortified base. They'd grab a few hours of sleep and do it all again the next day. I went back to the CNN office in the Palestine Hotel feeling as if the day had been a waste. The patrol had been uneventful. When I stepped inside, phones were ringing, producers were yelling into satellite phones trying to confirm information. There had been multiple coordinated attacks against Iraqi police stations in several cities. Dozens were dead. The headlines that night on American TV and in the newspapers the following day would be IRAQ EXPLODES.

At first I was pissed off that I had missed it, stuck on a patrol that had gone nowhere. Then I realized that there was a lesson to be learned about what gets covered, what we see about Iraq at home. Not all of Iraq had exploded that day, at least not the part of Baghdad I was in. The headline could just as easily have been "200 Gallons of Water Delivered to Neighborhood Near Baghdad Airport." It would have been just as accurate, though arguably not as important. Perhaps the soldier I spoke to earlier was right: sometimes Iraq is not like what you see on TV.

In Baghdad in 2005 the list of what you can't do is much longer than the list of what you can. You can't: eat in a restaurant; go to the movies; hail a taxi; go out at night; stroll down the street; stand in a crowd; stay in one spot too long; use the same route; get stuck in traffic; forget to barricade your door at night; neglect to speak in code when using walkie-talkies; or go anywhere without armed guards, communication devices, an ID, a Kevlar vest, or a multi-vehicle convoy. You can't forget you're a target.

Other than that, it's not so bad.

It's two days before the interim presidential elections, which will be either a milestone of democracy or a meaningless gesture, depending on what edge of the political spectrum you hang from. The security situation seems a bit better, but it's hard to know. There are more Iraqis manning roadblocks, but how good any of them is in a fight is impossible to tell.

There are true believers to be sure, holed up behind high walls and concertina wire, camped out in the "Green Zone," the most protected spot in the center of town: civilians and soldiers, planners and plotters, trying to respond to events on the ground. The Green Zone is a city within a city. Walled off.

Cut off. Miles of blast screens and barriers several feet thick. You meet with military officials there, and they give you briefings with bar graphs and pie charts: number of operations, number of insurgent attacks. It all seems so neat and clear, but outside the Green Zone it's anything but.

I'm in an up-armored Humvee, barreling down the center of a Baghdad street.

"Locals put shit out in the road all the time to slow us down," Captain Thomas Pugsley says.

Already tonight one soldier from his brigade has been killed, and another one is in the hospital undergoing surgery. "You lose soldiers, and it sucks, but you just have to drive on," he says, his eyes constantly scanning one side of the road, then the other. "I don't think there's a unit in this brigade that hasn't lost at least one if not more. It's always in the back of your mind when you go out, but you got a job to do and the whole highlight of our time here will be based on the outcome of these elections, so we're trying to put our best foot forward, and make the best of it we can."

Captain Pugsley's got a couple of platoons of Iraqi National Guard troops to check on. They're supposed to be guarding polling stations in advance of the elections.

"It seems calm," I say to no one in particular.

"It always seems calm until the first bullet flies by," a voice says out of the dark.

Captain Pugsley is with Alpha Battery, Fifth Brigade, First Cavalry. He's a field artillery unit battery commander, but Baghdad doesn't need those. It needs bodies on the ground. So after a brief "transitioning," Pugsley and his soldiers were rebranded mechanized light infantry.

"I thought it was going to be all frickin' desert," Pugsley says of Iraq, "but it's not." He interrupts himself every few seconds to shout instructions to his gunner, Specialist Chris Maxfield, who's sticking halfway out of the roof of the Humvee behind a fifty-caliber machine gun and clutching a spotlight.

"What do we got? Spotlight!" Pugsley also yells directions to his driver: "Go around! Watch it! Go wide left! Stay away from it!"

They are constantly on the lookout for IEDs, which are becoming ever more sophisticated and deadly. U.S. soldiers have found them hidden in abandoned cars, in garbage, even in the carcasses of dead dogs placed on the side of the road.

"We build it, they blow it up," Pugsley says, checking off in his head the list of recent attacks. "Our neighborhood advisory council building got blown up twice, our Iraqi police station got blown up on the same corner, and the youth center that the Iraqi government was building for the kids—someone blew that up too. We're rebuilding them all again."

"There's time it seems to get better, and then it just falls apart again," Specialist Maxfield tells me later, "and then you start over again, rebuilding, doing projects; then it goes back to the way it was before. I personally don't care. All I care about is going home."

Maxfield is twenty-four. He has only one more month to go; then he plans to get out of the army and go to college.

On patrols some officers try to sell you the story, upbeat West Pointers who've drunk the Kool-Aid and taken the class: Dealing with the Media 101. They focus on the big picture. Ask an enlisted guy how it's working with the Iraqis and he'll likely tell you, "They aren't worth a pile of shit." Ask an officer, it's usually a different story: "We're working well together with our Iraqi partners," they'll say. The truth is probably somewhere in between.

When we get to the polling spot, the Iraqi troops are freaked. They didn't think they'd have to stay out overnight, with no supplies. "I know it sucks," Captain Pugsley tells them. "We'll try to get some cots out to you and some flashlights."

A few blocks away, Pugsley notices one Iraqi soldier dancing. "Hey, get to work!" he yells. "You've got a job to do!"

"Anything that represents progress is a potential target," First Lieutenant Adam Jacobs tells me. He worries not just about the insurgents and the Iraqi forces, but also about keeping his young soldiers focused. "It's hard to keep them motivated," he says. "I just try to remind them that what they're doing—though it seems mundane at the time—is for a greater good. Just to sort of gain the bigger picture when they're on a rooftop staring at a road that there's not much traffic going down."

Riding along in the pitch black Humvee, you really have to admire these guys. Reporters can leave, fly home when they're done, but these young men and women are stuck for the long haul. They work around the clock. Countless patrols. No end in sight.

Outside another polling station, an Iraqi National Guard soldier, masked and alone, stares out into the darkness. The whites of his eyes dart about nervously; they are the only part of him visible beneath his black balaclava. Gunshots echo in the street.

Back at base, a camp called Victory, there's row

after row of trailers, a Burger King, and a giant PX. You can buy TVs, stereos, and T-shirts that ask WHO'S YOUR BAGHDADDY? You can also just stand in the aisles, close your eyes, and listen to the Muzak. For a moment it feels like America. It doesn't last long, but it sure does feel good.

By the Burger King, soldiers from all around the country lie about in a fast-food funk. A squad of reservists from Washington State sits in the shade of a trailer licking the last of the cheeseburgers off their fingers. They are dusty and dirty, their skin burned from days in the sun.

"This place sucks shit through a straw," one soldier tells me. I don't ask him when he's going home. He has no idea, so why rub it in?

When I first arrived in Sarajevo in 1993 I wore my Kevlar vest all the time. I even slept with it near my pillow. After a couple of days, however, I'd hardly ever put it on. I'd keep it with me in my vehicle, but I wouldn't bring it into people's homes. Surrounded by Bosnians who didn't have protection, I felt that it was inappropriate for me to stay sealed off. I wanted them to tell me their stories, risk exposing themselves to me. I couldn't ask that of someone if I wasn't willing to expose myself as well. Without the vest, I could feel the breeze on my chest, the closeness of another person, the sense of loss in everyone's embrace.

I met a young woman named Eldina when she was fetching water one morning at a local pump, a chore she had to do five or six times a day, shifting heavy plastic containers from hand to hand. She invited me to her home, a small walk-up apartment where she lived with her father and grandmother.

We sat in one room of their three-room apartment. The windows, covered in heavy plastic, buckled with the wind trying to rip through the high floor. The grandmother tended a fire in the stove.

On their windowsill, Eldina had placed a tomato. I remarked how beautiful it was. Plump and red, a startling sight amid Sarajevo's gray stones and rusted steel.

"Paradise is a tomato," her grandmother said, delicately picking up the ripe fruit. "Paradise is a tomato." Her eyes twinkled with the reflection of the wood burning in her small stove.

Eldina's father was slim, haggard, with a look I saw on many men's faces in the city that year. His hair was silver, oily, his index fingers stained from months of smoking at the front. He smiled only briefly, just long enough to show his teeth, then inhaled deeply on one of the cigarettes he always kept lit. Eldina's mother and sister had left Sarajevo. Eldina believed that they were somewhere in Europe with relatives, but she'd not heard anything from them in several months.

"It's not easy to raise a family," her father said, sounding defensive. "I'm trying to take care of food and electricity. I'm trying the best in the situation."

He was a driver before the war, and showed me a scrapbook with pictures from better days: family outings to the beach, a dinner party with candles and wine.

Eldina and her grandmother seemed strong. I felt they would survive. The father, I was not so sure about. He had a look I remembered seeing in my father the one time I was allowed to visit him in the hospital after his heart attack.

"The other day I saw my best friend on the Serb lines," Eldina's father told me. "I could have shot him."

"Did you?"

"No." He paused, a little embarrassed by the admission. "I was so shocked to see him there."

Eldina had dressed up for my visit. She'd taken off the speckled gray overcoat she was wearing when I met her and put on a sweater and a colorful scarf. She was wearing makeup, trying to hide the freckles on her face. She was pretty, and I imagined her laying out her good clothes before going to sleep the night before. She watched me while her father spoke, attentive to filling my cup, making sure I was comfortable. I tried not to look at her too often. There was a hope in her eyes that made me sad.

Eldina's boyfriend was a soldier. She showed me his picture; a stocky boy posing with a friend. Both were wearing heavy wool uniforms and pointing their guns at the camera.

"He's been missing for almost a year," she said as she looked at the photo. "Sometimes I dream he's a prisoner held captive in a camp."

"He's dead," her father told me later, with Eldina still in earshot. "People saw him die. They just never got his body back. He's probably still lying in a field somewhere near the front."

Eldina brought her baby over from his crib near the stove. Her boyfriend never saw his son. The thought kept going through my mind as I cradled the sleeping infant.

I wondered what my own little family would

have done in Sarajevo. Would my mother have been able to survive selling possessions piecemeal in the marketplace like so many women had to do as the war dragged on? Would I have been able to provide for her and take care of myself?

While I was getting ready to leave, I noticed that Eldina's grandmother was crying silently. I didn't see the tears at first—they blended with her pale white, wrinkled flesh—but I saw them glisten on the back of her hand as she wiped them from her face. She reminded me of my childhood nanny, May, crying as she said goodbye. May had helped raise me from the time I was born, but when I started high school, she had to find another job. I didn't want her to go, but there was nothing I could do. After she left, I couldn't speak for days.

I said goodbye to Eldina and her father, squeezed her grandmother's hand and wished her well. I left behind some deutsche marks on the tray and walked quickly down the steps, glass crunching in the grooves of my boots, hot tears burning my throat.

Baghdad's Yarmouk Hospital is gearing up for the January interim elections. Extra plasma, extra beds. In the back I find the staff washing blood off stretchers. I'm told I can stay at Yarmouk for no more than half an hour. A CNN security guard stands near me at all times, and out on the street, other armed guards watch the road. A suicide bomber targeted the hospital in September, killing six people and wounding twenty-two others. My guards aren't taking any chances.

Yarmouk has the busiest ER in Iraq, and by midday it's already packed.

"There was a car bomb this morning, an explosion at a police station. Some of them arrived here," Dr. Rana Abdul Kareem tells me as she checks the chart of a man screaming on a nearby gurney. He is taken out, and another patient is brought in. The wheels of his gurney cut a path through a pool of blood on the floor.

"This man here has multiple bullet injuries," Dr. Kareem says. "Another one is in the operating room, and there is another one lying there, and there were some people with superficial injuries we treated and discharged."

The man they've just brought in has been placed in the center of the room. Several nurses dab at a gaping hole in his leg. He was driving his car and got caught in a firefight. His blood drips in a Jackson Pollock pattern next to a bloody sandal lying on the floor.

I'm at the hospital to do a story about reactions to the upcoming elections, and to ask Dr. Kareem about the prospects for peace. I know what she is going to say, but still I have to ask.

"For god's sake, don't speak about peace here. Just don't speak about peace," she says, spitting the word out as if sickened by the aftertaste. "Maybe after ten years we will have some peace, but now we have forgotten about something called peace in Iraq."

Dr. Kareem is weary of cameras, sick of reporters asking questions, hinting at changes that never come. I start to ask her something else, and she stares at me, tired and angry. I realize I've seen that look before.

It was my first trip to Sarajevo. 1993. The first year of the war. A woman was shot crossing the street, near Sniper Alley. Strangers hailed a passing car and loaded the woman into its backseat. I followed them to the hospital and into the ER. The doctors allowed me to shoot footage for a while. They were well versed in the kabuki of cameras, but no longer believed that anything about the situation in Bosnia would change.

"What picture has not already been taken?" a man in the ER asked me. "What haven't you seen? What don't you know? What remains to be said?"

I apologized, and put my camera down.

"Thank you," he said. "I think it's better if we die in silence."

Initially, people wanted you to take their pictures, tell their stories. They thought it would make a difference, force America or Europe to act to end the bloodshed. "Sarajevo was a cosmopolitan city," everyone said. "It didn't matter if you were Muslim, Serb, or Croat." As the war continued, however, the divisions were clearer. No one seemed to talk about living together again. No one wanted to talk at all.

At the Kino Café, about twenty young men and women sat in a smoke-filled room watching an American Western. The sound was low; you could barely hear Lee Marvin and Charles Bronson, but there were subtitles in what used to be called Serbo-Croatian but was now referred to as Bosnian. The young men were thin, many of them dressed in army uniforms; the women were stylish, their clothes pressed, hair and makeup well thought out.

"We want to look nice if we die," said Slema. She was twenty-one and smiling, but only partially joking. "There's no use to think about the future now. It's Russian roulette. Any time a grenade can fall and we can all be destroyed."

"It's not the time to cry for deaths," her friend said. "We live too fast. Everything is forgotten. Not forgotten—you remember somebody who was shot—but you don't have time to think about it."

"What do you think about?" I asked.

"How to survive. You can't dream about tomorrow," she said. "No, just live now. You think, 'Now I am talking.' You can't say, 'Tomorrow I will visit my grandmother's.' It's not possible to say."

"All the people in Sarajevo have a bullet for them," Slema said, taking a drag on her cigarette. "All of them have their turn. They are just waiting for it. Wondering, 'when is my turn?'"

When I left Sarajevo the first time, driving to the airport, I had to slow down as I passed a crowd of worn men and boys gathered in a small clearing. Silhouetted against the high beam of a truck's headlights were two pit bulls locked in an embrace. One dog clamped its jaws on the other's neck. A few men yelled instructions, smoke pouring from their mouths in the cool night air. Most just watched. The fight didn't last long. The smaller dog was soon on its side, unable to breathe. The larger one's mouth was wrapped around its neck, waiting for it to suffocate. When the end was in sight, the victor clear, the dogs were pulled apart. One man clamped his hands around the nearly dead loser. Blood glistened between the man's fingers as he tried to hold the dog's throat together. Money was exchanged; the crowd moved to disperse. A convoy of Bosnian army trucks rumbled past, filled with young men on their way to the front. No one in the crowd even looked up.

The first time I came to Iraq for CNN, I spent two days traveling with Ambassador J. Paul Bremer, then America's top diplomat there. It was June 2004. Bremer was about to hand over power to the first interim Iraqi government, and was visiting northern Iraq, pressing the flesh one last time with Kurdish leaders.

Bremer was surrounded at all times by gun-toting guards, former Special Forces soldiers, now contracted to Blackwater, a private security firm. We had permission to be with Bremer, go everywhere he went, talk with him along the way, but the Blackwater guys didn't care. They kept elbowing away my cameraman, Neil Hallsworth, every chance they got. They seemed to take great pleasure in it.

"Just give me a reason," the head of the security detail told Neil repeatedly under his breath.

"A reason to what, shoot you?" I asked Neil when he told me what was going on.

"I think so," he said, laughing.

"Well, if he does shoot you," I said, "make sure you tape it, because it'll be the most exciting video we get today."

Bremer was always dressed in a business suit, with a starched shirt and French cuffs. His only concession to the dirt and dust of Iraq: the desert combat boots he seemed to wear at all times. He was constantly moving, surrounded by a gaggle of guards, young Ivy League aides, and old-school advance men. On one leg of the trip, I rode in a bus with his advance team. The head guy told me he used to work for the Bushes back in Texas, and now kept Bremer running on time. We were in a convoy of Kurdish police cars and buses that snaked along for what seemed like a mile.

"This is great. Really cutting a low profile with this one," the advance man said, laughing and staring out the window of the bus. On both sides of the highway, angry Kurdish motorists sat waiting for our caravan to pass.

"It's okay," the advance man jokingly yelled out the window. "It's John Kerry. Vote for Kerry!"

Nothing Bremer ever said was particularly newsworthy. He was, after all, a diplomat, and the dance he was required to perform didn't allow for dramatic moves. Once he was out, he'd write a book—saying that there hadn't been enough troops on the ground in Iraq—but while he was still there, he never said anything nearly so strong.

In the air, Bremer traveled in an armada of Black Hawks. The heavy rotors sliced the air, shaking the sky with the power of American might. Riding in a chopper, your body shakes so much that your skin starts to itch. The Black Hawk's doors are open, and your feet dangle out in the air, blast-

furnace heat bakes your face, sucking the mois-
ture from your lips. Bremer's choppers flew low,
some fifty feet off the ground, too close for a
rocket-propelled grenade to be effective, or so they
said. They'd pitch up over power lines, then plunge
back down, with the door gunner letting off a few
rounds just to make sure the gun worked.

In one Kurdish town, Bremer's security detail
got into an argument with Iraqi journalists. The
journalists stormed out, refusing to cover Bremer's
press conference. Bremer was going to sneak out
the back and escape, but his advance man realized
what a mess that would be, so he sent his boss out
to the Kurdish journalists and Bremer held an impromptu meeting with them in the hallway. In the
crowd, a teenager who'd just finished telling me
how great America was had his hand slapped back
by Bremer's security detail when the boy tried to
hand the ambassador a small Kurdish flag.

On our way back to Baghdad, I was told I could
sit next to Bremer in his Black Hawk. It was a
photo op: me sitting next to the big man. The truth
was, with the crush of the rotor, conversation was
nearly impossible. Besides, Bremer was wearing
ear plugs, and clearly had no interest in talking
with me. I ended up just smiling at him a couple
of times and watching as he signed commenda-

tion letters to hundreds of Coalition Provisional Authority personnel. An aide handed him batches of the letters, which he scribbled his signature on, his White House cuff links catching the late-afternoon sun. There were three Blackwater gunmen seated around us, and perhaps a dozen more in the choppers that followed. The guard next to me had a Maori tattoo on his arm and was reading a well-worn paperback. At first I couldn't see what it was, but as he turned a page, I caught a glimpse of the title: **How to Win Friends and Influence People.**

The day before Baghdad's 2005 interim presidential elections, Iraqi security forces are on heightened alert. Getting anywhere in the city is difficult because of all the roadblocks, and I spend a lot of time working out of the cluster of small houses that CNN rents in a heavily guarded neighborhood.

Sometimes the city doesn't feel that dangerous, but just when you think this, a bomb goes off or someone gets kidnapped. Sitting in the office you see the numbers come across your computer screen, an endless string of press releases that never make it on air: Three policemen kidnapped. One Iraqi soldier killed. A grenade tossed into a store. A surgeon shot to death outside his home. No names, just bodies. So many small acts of terror that, after awhile, you lose track of them all.

Most reporters stay at one of several large hotels. When I first came to Iraq, in June 2004, CNN stayed at the Palestine, but the security situation there kept getting worse, so we relocated. On the roof of the Palestine is a labyrinth of makeshift shacks, rented out by news agencies. Each allows reporters standing in them to have a backdrop of Firdos Square, where the Saddam statue was torn down. At night on the roof, with the bright camera lights in your face, you make a tempting target, and sometimes a security guard has to stand in the shadows, just off to the side, watching the street for signs of snipers.

There's a dingy gift shop in the lobby of the hotel, with tacky trinkets, dust-covered knives, and cheap tins. I once bought a few boxes with Saddam's picture on them, but most of the Saddam items were snatched up long ago.

The Palestine's elevators are snail slow, and while waiting for them, people exchange death tolls like pleasantries. The first time I rode in the elevator, a South Korean woman with Birkenstocks and a DV camera whispered to a tanned American with a silver pompadour, "Did you hear? Three Iraqis were killed. IED."

"Yeah, two policemen got killed in Mosul," he responded.

When I stayed in the Palestine in 2004, our security guards warned us one morning of a potential attack. "We have a report some people might come door to door, killing non-Muslims," one of the guards told me. It had happened in Saudi Arabia several weeks before, so the threat didn't sound too far-fetched.

"We have a plan," he told me confidently, and handed me two large pieces of wood. "Use these to barricade your door at night."

"Two-by-fours?" I asked. "Wooden two-by-fours? Don't you have something a little bit more hi-tech?"

He just shrugged and looked at me as if he thought me a wimp. Which of course, I was.

The attack never came, though the morning I left, insurgents fired on the hotel with rockets. They parked a bus loaded with mortars a few hundred yards from the Palestine. One hit the Sheraton, next door. Another, the nearby Baghdad

Hotel. The weight of the rockets tipped the bus over, however, and most of the arsenal exploded. Two Iraqi guards were injured.

I'd worried about getting my morning wake-up call, and though a rocket slamming into the building next to me wasn't exactly what I'd had in mind, it definitely got me out of bed in a hurry.

A few hours later, while I was on the tarmac boarding the plane, a mortar landed several hundred meters away. The impact was loud, the plume of smoke clearly visible.

"It's all right...it's all right," a teenage baggage handler said, laughing. I'm still waiting to see if he was right.

———————

On Election Day in January 2005, Baghdad is all but shut down. No cars, no traffic, roadblocks everywhere. In a small polling station, a local school, a line of men wait patiently to vote. American troops are on the roof of a nearby building; no sign of them though on the streets. The block is cordoned off. Iraqi National Guard soldiers man one checkpoint, Iraqi police another.

As I pass the barbed-wire barricade, a member of the Iraqi National Guard asks me to take his picture, proudly holding his American-made rifle. He is young, cocky, clearly proud of his service, the kind of soldier armies are made of.

"This weapon," he says to me, slapping his rifle, "has made men, who think they are big men with RPGs, run like women on Haifa street. I swear by God, I shall fight forever."

I smile and move on. A half-dozen cell phones sit on a cement block, confiscated from people going to vote. Cell phones are used by insurgents to detonate bombs, and therefore aren't allowed near voting booths.

It's quiet in the line of Iraqis waiting to vote. At the entrance to the school, a poster on the wall reads DO NOT LIVE IN FEAR. IF YOU HAVE ANY INFORMATION ABOUT TERRORISTS, YOU MIGHT BE QUALIFIED TO GET A REWARD.

When people have finished voting, they dip their index finger in a jar of ink, a sign that they have done their duty. As they emerge from the school, many hold up their fingers, smiling at my camera.

"It's worth all the bloodshed," a man says looking at his finger. "This is going to determine the future of a nation and the people. Voting is a very good feeling."

A woman dressed in black, her legs swollen with disease, is pushed in a wheelchair by her son. Her name is Badria Flayih and she is ninety years old. As I approach, she holds up her ink-stained finger.

"I wasn't scared at all," she announces, practically shouting. "I couldn't sleep last night, I was so excited to come here and vote. May God save all Iraqis: Sunnis, Shiites, Kurds. We are all Iraqis—one nation."

The line of men behind her breaks into applause.

Rewind. Soweto. May 1994. A crowd of women broke into applause when the polling station opened its doors. The line of voters wound through the sprawling South African slum, and from above I imagined a thick black snake, coiled amid the shanties and mud alleys. Elsewhere in Soweto I'd seen young boys and girls chanting slogans, dancing in small groups, but on the line there was patience. The women and men, the old and young, had waited so long already; a few hours more didn't seem to matter very much.

There were so many theories back then, about what would happen when black South Africans finally took power—rumors of a guerrilla war fought by white Afrikaners, fears of what black rule would really mean.

Several weeks earlier I'd seen a young man shot to death. I was at a demonstration by the Inkatha Freedom Party against the African National Congress. It was in downtown Johannesburg, before downtown had completely fallen apart. Snipers in nearby buildings let off a couple of shots into the crowd. No one knew where the shots came from or which way to run.

"You can just as easily run into a bullet as run away from one," a cameraman once told me. I didn't run at all.

There was pandemonium, chaos, but standing watching it all unfold around me, I could break it down into hundreds of separate actions and reactions, a thousand different moments. An enraged old woman used a stick to hit a fallen Mandela campaign poster promising A BETTER LIFE FOR ALL. A half-dozen South African police tried to batter down the door of a building, while a female cop gripped the trigger of her shotgun, scanning the windows looking for shooters. Down the street, Asian hookers who worked out of a storefront whorehouse stood on a balcony in low-cut tops, their breasts squeezed between their elbows as they leaned straight-armed over the ledge trying to see what was happening.

The boy was perhaps fifteen. Shot once in the chest, he lay motionless on the ground. One of his red sneakers was by his side—it must have fallen off when he was shot—the other sneaker was still on his left foot. It had no laces. Four black policemen in riot gear dragged the boy's body behind a concrete wall. His feet scraped the ground, and the remaining sneaker came off. The bullet hole in his chest was small, surrounded by just a thin trickle of blood.

After the shooting stopped, the police began covering the bodies with blankets or campaign posters—whatever they could find. I walked several blocks to a nearby store and bought bottles of soda and water. I sat on the curb and downed them one after the other. During the chaos, I'd forgotten that I was in the middle of a city. I'd forgotten everything about myself. All I felt was the rush, the adrenaline. Sitting on the street, I could still feel it. It took hours for it to fade.

I'd been on this corner before. Two years earlier I'd gotten out of a cab across the street. The white Afrikaner driver had been lecturing me about how blacks would never rule here.

"AIDS and public transportation will be the savior of Africa," he told me.

He had picked me up outside a butcher's shop on Rocky Street, where a sign read MEAT MARKET and the wall behind the counter was plastered with nude centerfolds.

"See, the black male has sex four to five times a week," the driver had said matter-of-factly, "whereas the white person gets by with one to two times a week. So with AIDS, it's going to solve the problem. Ninety-four to ninety-seven is the big die-off period. I figure if eighty percent of the blacks, and only twenty percent of the whites are infected, and most of them are drug addicts, homosexuals, and liberals, that'd rule out a future black government here."

I didn't argue with him. Everyone carried a gun in those days, and there wasn't any point. On Election Day in Soweto, I thought about that cabdriver, and I thought about the young man I'd seen shot to death. We like to think we can predict the future. We like to think we understand the present. I'm not sure we ever do.

Niger
NIGHT SWEATS

I close my eyes, pretend to sleep. Maybe I am sleeping. In Africa it's hard to tell. Coiled in a dirty sheet, sweat-soaked, my hair matted with the day's dust and grains of sand in my mouth, I dream about work, storylines, plots; I edit pictures in my head. I wake gasping for breath, unsure where I am. Niger. Rwanda. Somalia.

In Africa there are too many pictures, too many contrasts. You can't catch them all. It's like sticking your head out of a fast-moving car—you suffocate; it's too much to take in. Amputations. Executions. Empty beds. Shuttered stores. Crippled kids. Wild-eyed gunmen. Stripped-down corpses. Crashed cars. Mass graves. Handmade tombstones. Scattered ammo. Half-starved dogs. Sniper warnings posted like billboards. Buses and boxcars stacked at intersections. Old men in boxy suits walking to jobs that don't exist in offices that aren't there. It all blurs together. Desert. Mountain. Rice paddy. Field. Farmers bent over. Heads rise as you pass. Eyes follow eyes. Little kids run to the road, stand frozen, not sure if they should be happy or scared. They keep their weight on their heels so they can run back at the lurch of the car, the crack of a shot. Houses, whole towns, nothing but rubble—roofs blown off, walls burnt out, crumbled. Desiccated, eviscerated, gutted, and flayed.

At some point though, the disorientation fades. You put it behind you; go on. There is an adventure waiting. Life happening. It's not your life, but it's as close as you'll get. You want to see it all.

One minute you're there—in it, stuck, stewing in the sadness, the loss, your shirt plastered to your back, your neck burned from the sun—then you're gone, seatbelt buckled, cool air cascading down, ice in the glass. You are gliding above the earth, laughing.

I'm in Maradi, Niger. It's late July 2005. A few days ago, I was in Rwanda with friends on vacation. I'd gone to see the mountain gorillas and to tour the new genocide museum. Not everyone's idea of fun, perhaps, but I've never been very good at taking time off. I burn on beaches, and get bored really quickly. I had a couple of days left in Rwanda, and was watching TV in my hotel room, when a short report came on about starvation in Niger.

"According to a report by the United Nations, 3.5 million Nigeriens are at risk of starvation, many of them children," the news anchor said, then moved on to something else.

I called CNN to see if I could go. My travel companions were pissed off, but not all that surprised. They were used to my bailing out on them at the last minute.

"Why would you want to go to Niger?" one of them asked when I told him of the change of plans.

"Why wouldn't you want to go?" I responded.

"Um, because I'm normal," he said, laughing.

I wished I knew how to explain it to them. It's as if a window opens, and you realize the world has been re-formed. I wanted to see the starvation. I needed to remind myself of its reality. I worry that if I get too comfortable, too complacent, I'll lose all feeling, all sensation.

The next day, I was on a plane, on my way. I'd been relieved of the burden of vacation. I was in motion once again, hurtling through space. Nothing was certain, but everything was clear.

————————

By all estimates, Niger is one of the poorest countries in the world. Ninety percent of it is desert, and even in good years, most people here barely get by. The average Nigerien woman gives birth eight times in her life, and one out of every four children dies before he reaches the age of five. One in four. It's a staggering statistic, but not hard to imagine when you see how poor Nigeriens' diet is, and what little access they have to medical care.

Even for adults, the summer months between the planting of crops and harvest is a difficult time. Nigeriens call it the hungry season, when they rely on grain stored up from the previous year to get by. In 2004 there was a drought, followed by an invasion of locusts. Crops were decimated, devoured, so now it's 2005, and there's no grain stored up. People are foraging for food, eating leaves off trees.

When you land in Niger, by the time you reach the end of the runway, Niamey International Airport is nowhere to be seen. On either side of the tarmac, sand and scrub brush stretch to the horizon.

The gin-swilling British businessman sitting next to me on the plane stares out the window and bursts into tears. "They have nothing," he mumbles to no one. "The children are dying."

"What's your problem?" the Air France flight attendant asks as he saunters by.

"People are dying," the businessman repeats.

"I know," the attendant says. "People are dying every day, all over the world." He was tired of dealing with drunks.

It is hard to see the hunger at first. In Niamey, chauffeur-driven Mercedes glide down potholed streets. Businessmen and bureaucrats shuttle about, car windows firmly shut. A layer of dust seems to coat everything.

"This isn't a famine, it's a sham-ine," I hear one European reporter mutter in the hotel, concerned that the images he's gathered aren't going to be what his bosses back in the newsroom are expecting. That's how TV works: You know the pictures you want, the pictures you're expected to find. Your bosses will be disappointed if you don't get them, so you scan the hospital beds, looking for the worst, unable to settle for anything less. Merely hungry isn't good enough. Merely sick won't warrant more than a cutaway shot.

The hunger is there, of course—you just have to look close. On the drive from Niamey to Maradi are fields of corn, sorghum, and millet. Crops are planted, but harvest is a long way off, and there's little food to get families through until then. Adults can live off leaves and grass; kids need nutrients, and there are none to be had.

"It's not so bad," I say to Charlie Moore, my producer, and as soon as the words come out of my mouth, I wish I could take them back.

"It's bad enough," he responds, and of course he's right.

It's bad enough.

"It's pretty bad out there," the air force officer said as I was gathering my things. "Where are you staying?"

"I don't know!" I shouted, and it came out sounding scared.

"What do you mean you don't know? You can't just go to Somalia. Who do you work for?" I was worried he'd take my phony press pass, so I told him I was staying with an aid agency; I just wasn't sure of their exact location. The truth was, I didn't have anyplace to stay, and I didn't really work for anyone.

It was early September 1992, and I'd just landed in Baidoa, Somalia. I hadn't been to Sarajevo yet. Burma was the only fighting I'd ever seen. After **Channel One** bought my Burma footage, I lived in Vietnam for six months, taking language classes in Hanoi and trying to shoot more stories. When my visa expired, **Channel One** still hadn't offered me a full-time job, so I had to come up with another plan.

I was twenty-five, two years older than my brother would ever be. A day might go by when I didn't think about his suicide, but then I'd be walking on the street, and a stain on the concrete would remind me of blood, and I'd run into a nearby restaurant and throw up in the bathroom.

I used to see my brother in Vietnam. Someone would round a corner or catch my attention in a crowd, and for a few seconds I would think it was Carter.

One evening in Hanoi, a crippled beggar stopped in front of me while I was in a café. He stretched out a twisted limb, asking for money. I glanced up and saw Carter's face. Something about the gentle look in his eyes, the cut of his hair, the looseness with which it fell from the side of his head. The thought stunned me.

The beggar left, and I wanted to run after him, talk with him in case it **was** Carter trying to reach out to me. I didn't move from my seat, however. It was a crazy thought, and I never told anyone about it. I was embarrassed, worried that even thinking it was a sign of delusion.

It wasn't just people who reminded me of Carter. Once, I was eating at a food stall near my apartment in Hanoi and I noticed that the ceiling was made of pressed leaves. It looked just like a box covered with tobacco leaves that Carter once gave me for Christmas. The texture and color were the same. For a moment, I remembered him so clearly: the shape of his body, the color of his hair, the delicate thinness of his fingers. It had been four years since his death, and still nothing about it made any sense. Vietnam hadn't filled in the shadows I saw when I looked in the mirror, or eased the sadness that seemed to flow through my veins. I was hurting, and needed to be around others who were hurting as well. I wanted to dangle over the edge and remember what it was like to feel. I also needed a job. Somalia had seemed like a logical choice.

Famine was sweeping the Horn of Africa. Tens of thousands of people had already died of starvation, and millions more were threatened. Somalia had no central government to deal with the drought, just competing warlords with private armies and countless guns.

The famine hadn't yet become a major story. In some three months, the U.S. military would send troops, the American public millions of dollars in aid, and the broadcast networks their anchors. Hundreds of thousands of lives would be saved, but after that, things would get out of control. They often do. It started off being one thing, and ended up as something else. Peacekeepers became peacemakers. A humanitarian mission became a hunt for a Somali warlord. A Black Hawk went down. U.S. troops got killed. The whole thing turned to shit.

It started, though, with the starving. Thousands dying every day: mostly kids and old people, the ones without weapons or money, or families to fall back on. Roving bands of teens armed with guns and grenade launchers rode around in tricked-out "technicals," pickups with machine guns mounted on the back.

I hitched a ride on a relief flight that the U.S. military had just begun operating out of Mombasa, Kenya. In Baidoa as many as a hundred people were dying a day. The United States was shipping in sacks of sorghum on lumbering C-130 Hercules transport planes. The bags of grain were stacked on wooden pallets, kept in place by mesh netting attached to the plane's floor by cables. On my flight, a half-dozen young men with high-and-tight crew cuts lay sleeping on top of the sacks of grain.

"Who are those guys?" I asked the air force officer on board the flight.

"We call those guys the snake eaters," he said, whispering as though he were divulging classified information. "They set up on the ground and monitor the security of the runway."

A month earlier, stuck in Nairobi, waiting for my visa to clear, I'd gone to see a low-budget action movie, **Snake Eater II**, with Lorenzo Lamas. These guys looked far more businesslike than the muscle-bound star in that film. When we landed, the snake eaters were the first ones out the cargo door. They ran to the side of the airstrip and disappeared into the bushes.

The C-130 wasn't on the ground more than twenty minutes when it shut its cargo door and took off, leaving behind a few sacks of sorghum, the icy smell of airplane fuel, and me.

On the other end of the runway, a handful of aid agencies had parked their pickup trucks. On

top of one of the trucks, a young Somali sat strad-
dling a heavy machine gun. In the back, gnarled
men in soiled T-shirts stood around grinning,
gnawing on small green twigs that I'd soon learn
was khat, the favorite pastime of Somali men—besides arguing and shooting one another. Khat is
like an amphetamine. Chew it all day, as many do
in Somalia, and you'll end up edgy, strung out—
just the kind of qualities you want in a Somali gunman. Only a few flights of relief food were getting
into the country, but dozens of planes packed with
the bitter stimulant were able to land at airstrips
every day throughout the starving nation.

That day I arrived a couple of Western aid workers waited for the food sacks to be loaded up. They
all ignored me, and I was too shy to approach
them. Journalists, I'd later learn, were considered
a pain in the ass. They arrived at a story demanding transportation and food, not to mention information. Relief workers put up with them if they
were from a major network, and had big audiences
who'd make donations, but if you were just some
kid with a home video camera, then nobody really
wanted to make the effort.

When the bags of sorghum were loaded onto
the trucks, everyone took off, leaving me standing
on the side of the runway alone. There are times

when the reality of what you've gotten yourself into hits you like a brick dropped from a tall building. Standing by the airstrip in Baidoa was one of those times. I was in way over my head, and had just realized it.

I had a couple of thousand dollars in cash, a camera, some blank videocassettes, and a backpack filled with cashews, the only food I'd had time to buy before boarding the flight. I had no idea what I was doing or what I should do next.

———

It's late July 2005. In a makeshift hospital in Maradi, Niger, dozens of mothers sit with their children, waiting to see if they are malnourished enough to be saved. The hospital is run by Médecins Sans Frontières (Doctors Without Borders), a French relief group that won the Nobel Peace Prize in 1999. They are one of my favorite relief organizations because they fearlessly go to the worst places, and they seem far more efficient than the lumbering UN.

The hospital is a few blocks off Maradi's main drag. This is the third largest city in Niger, but that's not saying much. Even the capital, Niamey, is a backwater, and it's a ten-hour drive away.

To get into the hospital the mothers pass through a small metal gate guarded by two unarmed men. By dawn there's already a long line to enter. The women are wrapped in impossibly bright fabrics, a collage of color shocking against their desert black skin.

Weeks later, when I return to New York, an elegant lady stops me on the street and puts her hand on my arm. "Oh, Anderson, those women in Niger." She sighs, pausing to gather her emotions. "I mean, the fabrics. Where do they find them? Those colors. They must put so much thought into it."

The morning I arrive at the hospital, there are about a dozen mothers waiting with their kids outside the gate. A naked little boy with skin like an elephant's squats in front of his mother and shits. She wipes his wrinkled butt with a piece of cardboard from a box of medicine.

The mothers watch you enter, watch you come and go as you please, the color of your skin, the camera on your shoulder, the only entry pass you need. In the twitch of an eye, they've scanned your clothes, your eyes, read your intentions, your ability to help them. They don't beg; they know you're not here for that. They see the camera, the notepad; you can do nothing for them right away. Maybe in the long term you can help, they think, so they'll let you take pictures; but, really, they don't care. Their needs are immediate. Liquid. Food. Nutrients. Now.

Inside the compound, just beyond the gates, in the admissions tent, Dr. Milton Tectonidis examines a two-year-old boy clinging to his mother's breast.

"He's quite dehydrated," he says about the boy, gently pinching the skin of the child's left arm. The boy's name is Rashidu. His eyes are wide, and he looks right at Dr. Tectonidis.

"Usually in a kid you look for sunken eyes, and skin that doesn't come back, skin that stays folded," he says, barely pausing long enough to glance up. "In a malnourished kid, however, it's not a very useful sign. Because they're so scrawny, the skin always stays like that."

In his native Canada, Dr. Tectonidis might be mistaken for a drifter. His long hair is unkempt; his tall, thin body swims in the white T-shirts he always wears. He has worked with Doctors Without Borders for more than a dozen years, and in as many countries. He's treated tens of thousands of children, perhaps hundreds of thousands. He's lost count of how many he's saved.

"The very bad ones are in such shock, they don't

look at you like that," Dr. Tectonidis says, smiling at Rashidu's unblinking gaze. "But he's weak, so I'll keep him here."

The tent is crowded. About forty mothers with children sit on wooden benches waiting to have their children measured and weighed on a giant scale that hangs from a bar. The mothers say nothing. Only the children make sounds—coughing and crying, crying and coughing. A constant cacophony.

Dr. Tectonidis doesn't wait for Rashidu to get weighed. There's not enough time. Cradling the child in his arms, he takes him straight to the intensive care ward.

The UN had been warning about food shortages in Niger for months, but who pays attention to press releases? In this television age, nothing is real without pictures: starving kids, bloated bellies, sunken eyes—Sally Struthers stuff. Warnings don't get headlines, crises do. Malnutrition sounds so bland. Famine? Now that's a showstopper. The problem is, Niger isn't suffering from famine—not yet. Adults aren't dying, just thousands of kids. It's a food shortage, a hunger crisis, severe malnutrition—none of which will get you a spot on prime-time TV. The BBC was the first TV crew here; we came second. Most American networks don't even bother to show up.

"We saw it coming in February," Dr. Tectonidis tells me later. "We sent out a press release saying, 'Watch out! We need free food and free health care.'" February. Now it's July. Help is just starting to arrive.

"Maybe it was the tsunami," I say. "People unable to focus on more than one crisis at a time."

Dr. Tectonidis shakes his head. "It's always like this," he says. "The less politically important a country is, the longer the delay."

According to Dr. Tectonidis, the UN wants to raise a billion dollars for a reserve fund. That way, every time there's an emergency they don't have to go around begging, and exaggerating the scope of the problem. That's basically what they do now. The figure they've been using, the one I heard on the BBC—"3.5 million Nigeriens at risk of starvation"—is carefully crafted and somewhat misleading. You've got to read the fine print. "At risk"—that's the key phrase. What exactly does it mean? We are all at risk in some way, aren't we? If no aid arrives, if no attention is paid, 3.5 million Nigeriens could starve. True. But it doesn't work like that. Kids start dying, then some reporters pay attention—usually freelancers, men and women looking to make a name for themselves. They arrive first. Their pictures motivate someone from a network to come and do the story. Then more aid arrives. It's not a perfect system, but it's what the market will bear. The problem for Niger is that not enough people are dying. A few thousand children isn't enough.

Rashidu is laid out on a plastic mattress. In the intensive care ward, there are no sheets on the beds. It's too messy for that. The room is actually a tent several hundred feet long, with a single row of beds on either side. The mothers share the mattresses with their children.

When a child is severely malnourished, his body breaks down, devouring itself. The fat goes first, then the muscles, then the organs: the liver, intestines, kidneys. The heart shrinks, the pulse slows, blood pressure drops. Diarrhea dehydrates, the immune system collapses. Starvation doesn't kill the child; infections and disease do. No layer of fat between flesh and bone, nothing to pad the pain. His little heart simply gives up.

I'm standing by Rashidu's bed, watching doctors work to save his life. I feel useless, a bystander, doing nothing to help. I check on the cameraman, make sure he's getting tight shots of Rashidu's scared face. I think about how to incorporate Rashidu into the story I'm writing in my head, the one I need to get on air in a few hours. It all feels so stupid. More than stupid—it feels inappropriate. I'm a shark picking up the scent of blood. This little boy is dying, and there's nothing I'm doing to help, just taking pictures of his misery. I hold his tiny foot in my hand. It's swollen with fluid.

"It's water in the tissues," Dr. Tectonidis explains. "Sometimes it's only in the feet, sometimes the hands, sometimes even around the eyes. It's called kwashiorkor, and it was first discovered in Africa in the twenties, but it's been seen everywhere since, even in the concentration camps in World War Two.

"I think we'll get him," Dr. Tectonidis says, inserting a tube into Rashidu's nose. "We'll give him fluid, give him sugar right away. Just a little, because their heart overwhelms quickly. And we'll give him antibiotics. And milk. If he makes it through the first day or two, you'll see him running around in another week."

Rashidu is crying, but he has no tears. In his eyes there is only terror. He lies on his back, arms outstretched. He is naked and shivering. He looks like a tiny, wrinkled old man. When he cries, it sounds like a baby bird being smothered.

I ask the cameraman to make sure he's getting the audio levels right.

"Journalist, yes? Hello."

The voice was young, enthusiastic. I couldn't see who was talking, however, because when the pickup truck swerved to a stop in front of me, it had kicked up a cloud of dust that quickly surrounded me.

It was September 1992, and I was walking along what I hoped was the road into Baidoa, nervously chewing the inside of my lip, a habit I'd picked up from my brother when we were both little. I'd been in Somalia for less than an hour and was already lost.

If I worked for a major news organization I'd have had a vehicle waiting to pick me up when I arrived. But I wasn't working for anyone, and had been too intimidated to ask the relief workers at the airstrip for help before they drove off.

I'd noticed the outline of a pickup truck heading my way, trailing a large cloud of dust. As it got closer, I made out at least two Somali men in the back cradling AK-47s.

"Oh, good," I said to myself. "Alone on a road, with gunmen."

When the truck stopped and the dust had cleared, I saw a young Somali man walking toward me.

"Journalist, yes?" the young man repeated. He was wearing an oversize white T-shirt with I'M THE BOSS emblazoned on the front.

The boss was Saiid. A student in Mogadishu before his country imploded, he now made a living off starvation. He and his friends bought some guns, rented a truck, and offered one-stop shopping to visiting journalists: translation, transportation, protection. It was a package deal Mike Ovitz would have been proud to have put together. Around his neck, Saiid wore a pen from ITN, The British television network. He said he had just finished working for them. Technically, this gave him more journalism experience than me.

"Whatever you can pay would be fine," Saiid kept insisting, which threw up all sorts of red flags, but he was adamant—and he had all the weapons—so I climbed into his truck, and off we went.

On the windshield he'd taped a bumper sticker: I ♥ SOMALIA.

At first the town was a blur of brown—brown houses hidden behind high brown walls, mini forts barricaded from one another. On the main street were stores and cafés of corrugated tin, nearly all of them seemed shut down. People, some little more than skeletons, shuffled along or sat staring vacantly from behind soiled rags.

Gunmen careened around corners in pickup trucks, horns bleating, rarely slowing for the starving, who scurried out of their way. In one truck, a boy of perhaps thirteen sat atop sandbags with an olive green grenade launcher resting on his shoulder. In another truck I saw what appeared to be an improvised cannon.

There were no traffic lights, of course; the biggest guns got right of way. We had only two AK-47s, so we ended up braking a lot.

"Why don't you carry a gun?" I asked Saiid, seated next to me in the truck's cab.

"I don't carry a gun because I'm an educator guy," he explained. "Educator guys don't need guns."

Saiid's philosophy of survival was simple. "I aim for myself," he explained. "It's not hard here. I'm living well."

I didn't really know where to begin, but I figured the hospital would be a logical start, so I asked Saiid to take me there. A sign out front warned those entering not to bring weapons inside, but no one seemed to pay much attention to this rule. In the courtyard, several Somali men squatted, cradling their guns, their long sarongs hiked up around their knees.

"Do you think it's okay if I go in?" I asked Saiid.

"Of course," he said, not understanding my reticence to barge into an operating room. "You are American."

There were two rooms for surgery. Neither had running water or electricity, so operations were performed only in daylight, which came through an open window across from the operating tables. On the floor, a plastic bin overflowed with bloody gauze bandages and refuse. When I entered, I saw a young American medical assistant bent over a shirtless Somali man with multiple wounds on his legs and a bandaged arm.

The medical assistant's name was Raymond. He was a twenty-eight-year-old volunteer with the International Medical Corps, an American group similar to Doctors Without Borders. Raymond was not a doctor, but in Somalia that didn't matter. He was American, had medical training, and, most important, was here. That was enough.

He was Southern, handsome in a Tom Cruise sort of way, appealing as much for the attitude and accent he swung around as for his looks. Dressed in blue surgical garb, he wore a medical kit bandolier style around his shoulder. He'd been in Baidoa for three months and apparently was used to reporters barging in on his operations.

"Look, I don't snivel about what I can't take care of," he said, examining the man's open wound. "I do what I can do and don't worry about the rest. I don't have any nightmares. The floors are filthy, we have no running water, there's pus all over everything, everything is infected, everything. It's one of those things you never really know what it's like till you're actually here yourself. I mean, intellectually you can figure it out, but it's one of those things you need to be here to really experience. You know what I mean?"

I was beginning to.

Dawn Macray, a pleasant nurse with short blond hair, came into the room. "We had a bomb blast last night," she told me. "Fifteen casualties. Three died immediately. Today we've had multiple gunshot wounds, a couple of knife wounds."

"Are things getting better here, now that food supplies are being airlifted?" I asked.

"Better how?" she responded. "They're still killing each other."

Raymond moved into the next room to help a retired American doctor amputate another leg. The doctor appeared to be in her late sixties and wore a miner's lamp on her forehead for extra light. The Somali man's wife was trying to prevent the amputation.

"Look, I'd like to save his leg, but we can't do that," Raymond explained, as the Somali hospital administrator halfheartedly translated. "I'll tell you what, we won't cut off the leg, we'll just clean it up, but if he dies, it's her fault."

After this grim possible prognosis was translated for her, the man's wife stopped yelling, and shrugged. The amputation didn't take long.

"Everything's a challenge," Raymond said, as he moved to another patient. "You don't have enough supplies, you don't have enough equipment, you don't have enough time. You've got too many wounded, and a lot of them, you can't do anything for. You've got an infected leg, the bone is dying. If we were in the States, we could do something about it. But we can't do that here. You do the best you can with what you have."

When I came back to Baidoa several months later, I asked at the hospital for Raymond, but they told me he had gone back home. No one would say why.

In the intensive care ward of the hospital in Maradi, Niger, a four-year-old boy named Aminu lies on a bed. He is just a few feet away from two-year-old Rashidu, but is barely visible beneath a heavy wool blanket. Aminu whimpers softly. His mother sits on the bed slowly waving a fan over him to keep the flies away. Her name is Zuera and she is remarkably beautiful—high cheekbones, night black skin, and two small scars, parallel lines on either side of her face. They are tribal markings that were cut into her flesh when she was just a few days old. In some other place, she could be a fashion model, but one of her legs is deformed, twisted from a childhood bout with polio. She walks on her own, but with a slight limp, a small imperfection. In Niger, however, it makes her undesirable because she's less able to work. She is married to a grizzled old man, with whom she's had three children.

"Her parents were probably relieved someone would marry her," a nurse says in passing.

"Aminu came in with severe kwashiorkor," Dr. Tectonidis tells me, lifting part of the gray blanket off the boy's tiny body. He cries softly at the sudden exposure, but allows Dr. Tectonidis to examine his blistered flesh.

"Water in the tissues, water around the eyes. And his skin is peeling off, because of a zinc deficiency."

"He's getting better very fast," Dr. Tectonidis says to Zuera, smiling. "I'm sure we're going to save him, if he makes it through another day or two."

"You mean he could still die," I ask, surprised.

"Oh yeah," he says, handing Aminu a tiny sweet. "In an hour he can die if he gets too much bacteria in his blood, despite our antibiotics. But he's had five candies already, and he drinks all his milk. That's the best sign."

The "milk" is a nutritional supplement created for severe malnutrition. It is filled with vitamins, Dr. Tectonidis says, the result of thirty years of research into the science of starvation.

"Before, we would stuff them with food, and half would die," Dr. Tectonidis says. "We learned they have to go slow in the beginning, if they're a

severe case. Don't give them iron in the beginning. Don't give them too much food. All these
things were learned by trial and error."

He holds a cup of the milk formula to Aminu's
lips, and the boy drinks it eagerly.

"What a life," the doctor says, his face just a few
inches from Aminu's. "What a life, eh, bambino?"

A few beds down from Aminu is Habu. He's ten
months old and close to death. Even I can see that.
His eyes are unfocused, his chest rattles as it rapidly rises and falls. I can actually see the outlines
of his heart beating beneath his paper-thin skin.

"He did well for a couple of days, but then on the
twenty-third he crashed," Dr. Tectonidis says, showing me Habu's chart. "He was admitted on the
nineteenth of July. He got an infection. Today is the
thirtieth, and he's worse than when he came in."

Habu's mother says nothing. She sits staring
off into the empty space between Dr. Tectonidis
and me.

"Will he make it?" I ask.

The doctor doesn't answer.

Here they treat the worst cases first. That's what
TV wants as well. The illest, the greatest in need.
It's a sad selection process that happens in your
head.

"That child's bad, but I think we can find worse,"

I say to myself, deciding whose suffering merits time on TV. You tell yourself it's okay, that your motives are good—at the moment you might even believe it. But later, alone, lying in bed, you go over the day and feel like a fraud. Each child's story is worthy of telling. There shouldn't be a sliding scale of death. The weight of it is crushing.

They die, I live. It's such a thin line to cross. Money makes the difference. If you have it, you can always survive, always find a place to stay, something to eat. For the first few days in Maradi, I'm not even hungry. It's not just the heat, the dust. I've become disgusted with myself. My body fat, my health, my minor aches and pains. I brought with me a bagful of food—cans of tuna and Power Bars—but the thought of eating anything makes me want to throw up. That changes, of course. After a couple days I forget why I'm depriving myself.

They die, I live. It's the way of the world, the way it's always been. I used to think that some good would come of my stories, that someone might be moved to act because of what I'd reported. I'm not sure I believe that anymore. One place improves, another falls apart. The map keeps changing; it's impossible to keep up. No matter how well I write, how truthful my tales, I can't do anything to save the lives of the children here, now.

The next morning when we come back to the intensive care ward, Habu's bed is empty. It's been some fifteen hours since we first met him. His mother is nowhere to be seen.

I find Dr. Tectonidis and ask him what happened. He doesn't remember who Habu is, but when I show him the empty bed, he checks the chart.

"He died this morning," he says, reading the nurse's notes. "They transfused him, but he was probably infected with something. They often come with malaria and bacterial infection. I knew yesterday he wouldn't make it. We tried. I gave him the blood—that was the one chance he had. And he made it through the night, but gave up."

Overall, only about 5 percent of the children the doctors treat here end up dying, but in the intensive care ward, there are two or three a day.

"There are some surprises," Dr. Tectonidis says. "Those are harder because we're a bit upset when it happens. But most of them we can tell. Then there are the miracles. We think they're going to go, and they make it. The worst ones are the ones we think are going to be okay and they drop suddenly. But the ones that we know, what can we do?"

"Don't you get overwhelmed?" I ask, already knowing the answer.

"We can't think too much about one of them," Dr. Tectonidis says, waving a hand. "The little kids they go easy. One in four of them. They estimate something like two hundred thousand children under five die a year here. And in a year like this, it's probably much more.

"I tell the nurses, 'If you get attached and you want to cry, fine—but go somewhere else. Go hide.' If you cry in front of the mothers, what good is that? It's not a sign of sympathy. It makes the other mothers worried. They start wondering, 'What's going to happen to my kid?' You can't do that; it's not fair. They look up to you like a God. You're the one chance they have. Only fifty people died here last month. We saved about fifteen hundred. You can't stop for one death. The mothers understand. They don't expect sympathy, they expect you to try your best. They don't expect you to cry for them. That's not your job."

I'd initially come to Somalia in 1992 on my own, hoping to get a job with **Channel One.** I wasn't prepared for what I saw. At outdoor feeding kitchens set up by international relief groups, young and old, like human skeletons, sat in rows waiting for food. The food was cooked in old, giant oil drums over charcoal fires. The smell of cooking food filled the air, taunting the hungry.

When a person died, he was wrapped in a shroud, and placed with the other bodies stacked like cords of wood in a makeshift morgue, eventually to be buried in an unmarked pit. Saiid took me out to the burial grounds, where each day dozens of graves were filled, while new ones were dug.

By the time we got there, it was already late in the day. I took some pictures of the graves, and then started to get worried because we were all alone. Just me and Saiid and two gunmen. I began to think that they might shoot me and dump my body in an empty grave. I couldn't imagine why they wouldn't. I had more money than I planned on giving them, and we hadn't discussed their fee.

"Saiid, did I mention that I have several journalist friends who will be coming to Baidoa in a couple of days?" I asked him, trying to come up with reasons he should keep me alive. "They'll need interpreters, and I will definitely give them your name."

I also gave him a raise on the spot.

We drove around aimlessly for a while, and ended up in a small gathering of makeshift huts along a dusty footpath, where a man and a woman squatted over the body of their dead child, lying on the dirt floor of the hut. I wasn't sure if I should videotape them. I didn't want to disturb their grief. When the man finally looked up, I motioned to him with my head, nodding toward my camera. He nodded back, and returned his attention to his son. I pressed RECORD.

The man appeared old, but was probably no more than forty. The boy had just died. The man held the boy's head in one hand and with the other spread out a dirty cloth to cover the child's face and body. The woman filled a kettle with what little water they had. Slowly, sparingly, she poured it over her son. You could see his hollowed-out eyes through the wet cloth; his ribs were visible as well. He had no muscle, no fat. His legs were as thin as the sticks that formed the outer layer of the hut.

They had already watched their three other sons die. This was their last. He was five years old.

He was just one boy, his was just one death. It

happened a thousand times a day in places like this all over Somalia. It happened every day.

———————

"Aminu's dead."

Charlie Moore, my producer, tells me when he gets back from the intensive care ward. Aminu was four. Yesterday he seemed better. Yesterday was a long time ago.

"Aminu's dead."

That's all the nurses said. They don't know exactly what killed him. They don't do autopsies here in Maradi. No point. No time. Aminu was starving, but that's not what finally did him in. He'd been sick for months, hospitalized for the last two weeks. His body was riddled with infections. He might have had malaria; his skin was peeling off.

"Aminu's dead."

When Charlie tells me, I'm surprised at how shocked I am. We both knew this could happen; it's just not what I expected. It seems so unfair. Dr. Tectonidis had been optimistic. Aminu had been eating sweets, drinking his milk formula.

He'd made it through the worst of his illness. He was going to be our success story, a bundle of hope to end our report after the death of Habu. We both know what this means. We find our cameraman and head back to the hospital. That's what we're here for, after all, to document the death. That's how it works, isn't it? Tell stories, get pictures, look out for just such poignant moments. It's not pretty how poignancy is made.

At the hospital, Aminu's bed is empty. His mother, Zuera, left this morning.

"When there's bed pressure, they throw them out faster," Dr. Tectonidis explains. "When there's no bed pressure, they tend to keep them a bit."

Aminu was buried a few hours after he died. Women are not allowed in the cemetery, so Zuera didn't see her son's body wrapped in white cloth and deposited in the sandy soil like an oversize seed hastily planted in the earth. There was no service, no headstone. Nothing marks the grave. A little mound is all that remains. We go and video-tape it, but it barely reads on camera.

When a child dies at night in the intensive care ward, the nurses let his mother sleep by his side. I can't get this image out of my mind. Did Zuera speak to her baby in the pitch black of night? When she opened her eyes in the morning, did she think

1

2

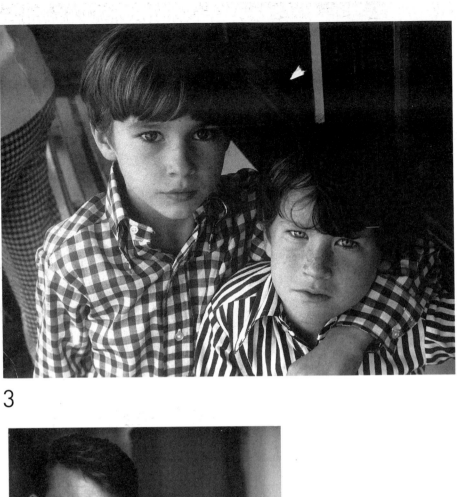

3

4

5

6

7

8

9

10

11

12

13

14

15

16

he was still alive? How many seconds was it before she remembered?

Aminu's dead.

––––––––

It takes us half a day to find out where Zuera lives, another half day to get there.

It's a small village in the midst of a cornfield. A collection of thatched huts and mud homes. When we arrive, Zuera is sitting outside her one-room house, in a courtyard surrounded by women, their feet splayed out in front of them.

Her elderly husband is there as well, standing in a group of men, off to the side. No one seems particularly surprised that Aminu has died. There is no crying, no wailing. Death has come to this village before. Aminu is the first child Zuera has lost, but nearly every mother here has lost at least one child.

"He was a good boy, a gentle boy," Zuera says softly. "They tried their best for him." She holds her youngest child, Sani, in her arms. He is two and doesn't understand what's happened to his brother. "He was always with Aminu," Zuera says. "This morning he kept calling out his name."

Behind her, two women stand over waist-high wooden mortars, pounding millet into flour. The dull thud of the pestles, one after the other, the steady pulse of village life. I pick up a wooden pestle, shiny smooth at either end from years of sweat and scraping. It's heavy and hard to imagine anyone wielding it day after day. The women laugh when I pretend to be too weak to hold it.

Nearby, Zuera's grandmother sits with three other elderly women, picking at a bowl of dried leaves—the staple of their diet for months.

Aminu is the thirteenth great-grandchild of hers to die. Half of her thirty-eight grandchildren have died as well. She can't even remember all their names.

Inside Zuera's one-room house is a twin bed with a thin mattress—little else. I've been in dozens of homes like this over the years, and every time, I still find it shocking. A dirt floor, makeshift shelves. The only decoration: some torn pages from an old magazine taped to one of the walls. Zuera has more than most—the benefit of having an older husband, perhaps—but I can't imagine what her life is really like. The few pieces of clothes Aminu wore will be given to his little brother. There are no pictures of any of the children. Photos are expensive, and Aminu was too young. Zuera will have nothing to remember her dead son by. None of the mothers ever do. The pictures we've taken of Aminu and Habu and the others are likely the only images that will ever exist of them. The only markers that they were ever alive.

———————————

I boarded the plane in Baidoa, soaking wet with sweat. I'd been in Somalia less than forty-eight hours but had shot enough material for two reports and needed to return to Nairobi to write them. I was dehydrated and running a high fever.

I'd finished off the last of my water the previous night. The Red Cross had let me stay in their guarded compound. I'd slept on the floor and considered myself lucky.

When the C-130 finally took off, I leaned back. Cool air blew out of a pipe in the roof, and the plane quickly got cold. I shuddered with the change of temperature.

One of the airmen removed a cassette tape from

his flight suit and disappeared toward the cockpit. Seconds later, Queen's "Bohemian Rhapsody" began to blare from speakers near my head.

"Is this the real life? / Is this just fantasy? / Caught in a landslide / No escape from reality." I looked out a side window, trying to catch one last glimpse of Baidoa.

"I always wanted to pee over the equator," one of the airmen said. He unzipped his flight suit and leaned against a pouch on the side of the plane, which allowed his urine to trickle out into the clouds. The pilot began to rock the plane back and forth, making it difficult for the airman to keep his balance. Everyone laughed.

I arrived back in Nairobi and showered the dust from my hair, lathered my body, pried the dirt from my finger- and toenails. I put on fresh clothes, went to an Italian restaurant, ate pasta, drank passion fruit juice, watched the TV above the bar. I'd been there, now I was here. A short plane ride, a few hundred miles, another world, light years away.

I finished my meal. A cool breeze blew through the restaurant. When I breathed deeply, however, I was suddenly assaulted by a smell. Smoke, rot, flesh, and food—it was the smell of Somalia, and it came like a stiletto stab out of the shadows. I couldn't tell where it was coming from. My clothes were clean, so was my skin. For a moment I thought it was my imagination, a hallucination brought on by the heat and my fever. Then I realized that it was coming from my boots. I had only one pair, and the smell of that place had soaked into the leather, worked itself into the soles. Just that morning, in Baidoa, getting pictures of a dead donkey, I'd stepped into a pool of blood. Who knew what else I'd walked through?

Every story has a smell. I don't always notice it at first. Sometimes it takes days before it weaves itself into the fabric of my clothing, and sinks into some dark corner of my cortex, becoming memory. I come home, I can't smell a thing.

That night, lying on the well-worn mattress in my dingy room, listening to the tap drip and the mechanical laughter of the **matatu** minibuses on the street outside, I cried. It was the first time in years.

———

Somalia got me a full-time job as a correspondent with **Channel One.** That's what I'd wanted.

That's what I'd been hoping for. When I actually got it, however, it didn't feel so good.

The pictures of the man and woman washing the body of their dead child caused a stir among many schools that aired **Channel One** in their classrooms. Some schools held raffles and bake sales to raise money for Somalia relief.

"I'm building a career on the misery of others," I said to a friend.

"You're not doing that," she told me. "You're informing others about the plight of people who are suffering." Perhaps—but the irony was, the more sadness I saw, the more success I had. After I got back from Somalia, **Channel One** gave me a two-year contract.

In Somalia, the relief flights continued for several months, but it became clear that much of the food wasn't getting to the starving. Once it left the planes, it was ripped off by the warlords who ruled the streets. The U.S. military announced plans for a humanitarian mission, to secure the distribution of aid—Operation Restore Hope they called it. In December 1992, some three months after I'd first gone to Somalia, **Channel One** asked me to go back, so I could be there when U.S. troops landed.

I flew to Somalia's capital, Mogadishu, a crumbling city of shell-pocked villas, streets strewn with torn-up pavement, and lights that hadn't worked in years. The main hotel in Mogadishu was fully booked for the invasion, taken over by dozens of international journalists. Satellite dishes covered the roof, a few scattered mattresses lay in halls for those like me, unable to find rooms.

It was the first time I saw the U.S. military and the U.S. media in action up close. American troops came ashore under the glare of camera lights, broadcast live around the world. Soon after, the military sent in its public affairs officers, PR troops waving lists of free rides on choppers and tours of ships, for journalists desperate to file a story. It seemed that everybody was spinning in those days, crafting the message for mass consumption. Photo ops, exclusive sit-downs, walkabouts. Uncle Sam gave you access if you made a deal.

It was a game you could get trapped in. You needed them because they controlled the scene; they needed you because they wanted their message out. They fed you, you ate it up, and tried not to soil yourself along the way.

Several days after the invasion, I rode on a chopper out to the USS **Tripoli**—just me and a newspaper reporter and photographer.

"What do you think about this?" the navy press officer yelled to the print reporter, above the din of the helicopter. "The entire crew of the **Tripoli** on deck spelling out 'Thank you, America'?"

"Sounds like a front-page photo to me," she said, grinning.

Somalia had its own rules, its own codes, very different from our own. All I saw the first time was the starvation, the gunmen, but the picture was far more complex. There was an order to it; I just didn't realize it at first. It was like walking into a darkened theater; it took time for your eyes to adjust.

In the beginning, Somalis seemed thankful that the U.S. military had arrived, but the longer we stayed the less welcome we all became.

One day, a French military jeep stopped in front of the hotel; the squeaking of brakes got my attention. A Somali woman wrapped in bright fabric got out of the passenger seat. Out of the swirl of the street a hand grabbed her. Someone called her a whore. The crowd seemed to gel. Fists and feet thrust at her; she twisted about. She may have cried or tried to explain, but I couldn't hear her above the yells of the mob. The men in back pushed for a better view, jostled for their chance to strike.

The woman spinned, grabbed a knife from one of the watermelon sellers outside the hotel entrance. I climbed onto the wall of the courtyard and turned on my camera. With one eye I peered through the viewfinder at the woman in grainy black and white striking out at the crowd with the knife. With the other eye, I watched, in color, the men laughing as she tried to fend them off. She was close, just below me. Between us there was only a parked car. I could have jumped down, tried to lift her to safety. I thought about it, but did nothing. I worried that the mob would grab me as well, or that I might make things worse for her by intervening. Maybe I was just scared.

Someone took the knife away from her; her top got ripped, exposing one of her breasts—a shocking sight in this covered-up culture. A convoy of U.S. marines drove by; they slowed to honk at the crowd. A few marines craned their necks to see what the commotion was about, but the crowd let them pass. The convoy sped on.

A pipe whizzed past my head, landing in the courtyard behind me. Some Somalis began yelling at me and at a couple of other reporters who were watching. They didn't want us taping them.

I suppose I should have stopped then, climbed down from the wall. I knew the video probably wouldn't make air—the attack was of no real consequence—but that didn't matter to me at the time. I thought that by taping this attack, I was somehow taking a stand, showing these men that they were being watched, that people saw and cared what they were doing. It sounds so foolish now.

I closed my outer eye and watched through the viewfinder, detached in black and white as the men faced me, shouting, waving their hands, shaking their fists. It was silent, as I remember it; my only thought: Whom should I focus on? I once heard about a police officer who'd responded to a domestic dispute in a housing project. When he walked into the apartment there was a man pointing a gun at him. The cop knew that if he moved, the man would shoot, so he released all the tension from his body and projected nothing. No fear, no hostility, no threat. He thought of himself as invisible, and the gunman left. Standing on the wall, looking through my camera's viewfinder, I felt as if I weren't even there.

Finally, someone grabbed my legs from behind, tugging at my jeans. It was another reporter inside the courtyard.

"Get down," he yelled, and I started to lower

myself from the wall. Before I dropped, I looked for the woman. I caught just a glimpse of her. She was being led away by several men in the crowd. I never found out what happened to her. I never saw her again.

For the next two years, I traveled continually for **Channel One.** Bosnia came next, then Croatia, Russia, Ukraine, Georgia, Israel, Cambodia, Haiti, Indonesia, South Africa. Wherever there was conflict, I wanted to go.

In May 1994, I headed to Rwanda. The genocide was well under way. Hundreds of thousands of Rwandan Tutsis and sympathetic Hutus had already been killed. Many more would die before it was over. The mostly Tutsi army of the Rwandan Patriotic Front was advancing on the capital, Kigali. They were on the verge of victory and had vowed to stop the killings. Hundreds of thousands of Hutus were streaming for the borders. With blood on their hands, they slinked into Tanzania and Zaire, hoping to lose their sin in the crush of the crowd. Their piles of weapons were the first thing you noticed when you crossed into Rwanda. The weapons and the bodies.

Most were naked, swollen grotesquely by gases and water. There were at least a dozen of them, bobbing up and down, at the base of a small waterfall underneath the bridge you had to cross to get into Rwanda from Tanzania. It was hard to count how many; they twisted and turned in the tide, their arms flailed about in the churning water. I noticed the body of a child stuck between two rocks. His arms shook as waves of water washed over him. I watched him for several minutes. I couldn't look away. I kept wondering if his body would somehow become dislodged, break free. It never did. Not while I was there, at least. Breathing on the bridge was difficult. When I opened my mouth, the spray from the falls filled it with the taste of rotted flesh.

The bodies floated downstream, about one a minute. I actually stood there and timed them. I heard that thousands of bodies floated all the way to Lake Victoria in Uganda, where the UN paid locals a dollar a corpse to fish them out.

The border was controlled by the Rwandan Patriotic Front. When I first approached them, I tried to be diplomatic.

"I'd like to see some of the local areas," I explained to a soldier in army green fatigues and red Converse hightops.

He looked at me as if I were an idiot. "Don't you want to see the massacres?" he asked. The rebels knew all about the value of good public relations. "We will help design a program that meets all your needs," he promised.

His name was Lieutenant Tony. He took us into Rwanda the next day.

I'd rented a car in Tanzania, but I didn't tell the driver where we were headed because I was afraid he wouldn't go. I said we were just driving to the border. The joke was on me, though. Since he didn't think we were going far, he didn't fill the tank with gas. We had only a few gallons. So every time we passed a rebel vehicle, we had to stop and beg them for a few liters of fuel.

"Please, we have a war to run, you know," Lieutenant Tony complained whenever we stopped for gas. "We don't have much petrol left ourselves. We can't give it away."

"We'd be happy to buy some," I said.

"Please, let's continue," he responded.

That's how our conversation went for several hours.

You smelled the bodies before you saw them, but the truth is, after a while, you stopped seeing them altogether. Even monstrosities can become mundane if you stand too close.

On the side of a road we came upon five bodies. They were lying in a row, partially hidden in a field of grass. For a moment, I thought maybe they were only resting, a family that had stopped to nap on their way to market. They were dead, of course. Exposed to the elements, they seemed to have shrunk, their skin stretched over their bones like leather. There was a little girl. I could just make out tufts of hair on her withered scalp. Next to her was a woman in a dirty white blouse. Her hand rested on the man she lay next to. At first I thought she was wearing a glove. It seemed partially removed. Then I realized that it was her skin. Hardened by the sun, it had peeled off. So had the soles of her feet. I'd never seen anything like it. Her face had decomposed as well. Her teeth were visible still attached to her jaw. She appeared to be smiling.

No one said anything. We stood listening to the buzzing of flies and the cries of a vulture circling overhead, waiting for us to leave.

"Bastards," my producer muttered, as he looked over the scene.

I remember thinking how strange it was that he said that. He was cursing the people who had done this, I knew that, but I thought it odd that he was taking it so personally. I didn't realize that I was the odd one for not doing so.

I stepped over the bodies, bent down, took out my cheap instamatic camera, and took close-up pictures of the woman's hand. Click. Click. Weeks later, when I got the photos developed, the clerk in the drugstore looked at me, disgusted. When I saw the photos, I understood why. I'd crossed some marker, stepped over a line. The corpses were mixed in with pictures of smiling soldiers and of my camera crew, souvenir snapshots I'd taken for my scrapbook. At the time I'd seen nothing inappropriate about this. But later I realized that it was time to stop, time to seek out other kinds of assignments.

In Somalia, when I'd started my career two years before, each body came as a shock. I used to imagine the lives they'd led. The father coming home from work, perhaps a teacher. The mother raising the children. I pictured them alive, around a table, talking about their day. That, for me, was always the saddest part. The fact that no one would re-

member their passing. Their history, their squab-
bles, the joys they'd experienced—all of it just
dissolved with their bodies on the side of a road.
They'd simply disappeared.

In Rwanda, however, I no longer thought about
who these people were. I was transfixed by the
details of their death. Fascinated with the stages
of decay, the surprise of rigor mortis, I'd forgotten
what I was really looking at.

The more you've seen, the more it takes to make
you see. The more it takes to affect you. That is
why you're there, after all—to be affected. To be
changed. In Somalia, I'd started off searching for
feeling. In Rwanda, I ended up losing it again.

"My heart is too full," I told my boss soon after I
got back. I didn't want to see any more death. I
think he thought I wanted more money, but the
truth was, I'd simply had enough. Months later my
contract with **Channel One** expired, and I decided
to leave. I got an offer from **ABC News.** I was in-
credibly flattered, but I also thought it was funny. I
hadn't been able to get an entry-level job at ABC in
1992. Just three years later, they were asking me to
become a correspondent. They told me I'd be working mainly in the United States, which was fine by
me. I needed to stop searching the world for feeling. I needed to find it closer to home.

Katrina

FACING THE STORM

It begins as a breeze, barely noticed, brushing the land where man was born. A bush pilot flying out of Kisangani might have found himself buffeted by a surprisingly strong current of air, or a farmer on a rocky Rwandan slope stretching his back as he stood could have felt the cool wind on his face. But it's not until the third week of August 2005 that meteorologists take note of a powerful tropical wave of wind and water moving slowly off the coast of West Africa. It crosses the Atlantic and feeds off the warm waters of the Bahamas, growing in size and strength. On August 24 it becomes a tropical storm, and automatically is assigned the next name on a list created by the National Hurricane Center: Katrina.

I'm on a boat with friends off the coast of Croatia, sailing in the crisp blue waters of the Adriatic.

This is my second attempt this year to have a vacation, after cutting short my trip to Rwanda in July to go to Niger. I've resisted checking my e-mails for several days, but my BlackBerry is on and when it begins to ring, I know it's not good.

"Sorry, buddy, but you need to come back," David Doss, my executive producer, tells me.

Katrina becomes a hurricane on Thursday, August 25, and that evening it hits southern Florida. Twelve people die. Over land, the storm weakens, but once it returns over water, this time the Gulf of Mexico, it begins to re-form.

Saturday morning, I fly out of Dubrovnik, bound for Houston. In Louisiana, New Orleans mayor Ray Nagin and Governor Kathleen Blanco hold a press conference, asking city residents to leave. Nagin and Blanco don't, however, make the evacuation mandatory. That evening, Max Mayfield of the National Hurricane Center calls the mayor to warn him personally of the seriousness of the storm. It's only the second time he's called a politician to do that.

New Orleans' emergency plan requires authorities to provide buses to evacuate the one hundred thousand residents without access to transportation. No buses, though, are organized to get people out of the city. On Sunday, over the central Gulf of Mexico, Katrina turns northwest as expected, becoming a monstrous category 5 hurricane. Sustained winds 175 miles per hour. The mayor and governor finally declare a mandatory evacuation.

I arrive in Houston late Sunday and drive to Baton Rouge. I get there around 1:00 A.M. on Monday, just as the outer bands of rain are beginning to hit. It's another hour-and-a-half drive to New Orleans, but when I call into my office, they tell me that the roads are closed. I am furious with myself for getting there late, but it turns out that CNN has pulled its satellite trucks from New Orleans because they anticipate flooding. Even if I were able to get there, I couldn't broadcast during the storm, so I decide to ride it out in Baton Rouge, then head to New Orleans as soon as it's over.

Katrina is the sixth major hurricane I've covered in the last fifteen months, the second one this year. I never used to understand people's fascination with the weather. One of the great joys of living in New York is that I'm able to ignore what little bit of sky I ever see. Since covering Hurricane Charley in 2004, however, I've continually volunteered to report on hurricanes. It's not just the storm itself that I find compelling, but also the hours before and after. There is a stillness, quietness. Stores are shut, homes boarded up. In many ways it feels like a war zone.

A few hours before Hurricane Charley made landfall, I checked into a waterfront hotel in Tampa, Florida. The manager, a large woman with a small parrot perched on her head, agreed to let me stay if I signed a waiver absolving the hotel of any responsibility for my safety. As I signed the paper, the parrot defecated on the woman's shoulder.

"She's just a little nervous about the s-t-o-r-m," the woman said, spelling the word out, worried the parrot would hear.

Reporting on a hurricane, you depend on your skills for survival; it's all in your hands. You rent an SUV, load it up with water, food, whatever supplies you can buy; gas cans, coolers, and ice are always the hardest to find. In a war, you head to the front; in a hurricane you head to water. You pick your location as if you're planning an ambush. You want a spot near the water, so you can see the storm surge, but you need to be on high ground so you don't get flooded when the water rises. You don't want too many trees or signposts near you, because they can become airborne and turn into flying missiles in high winds. You also

need several fallback positions so that as the storm intensifies, you can retreat to ever more secure locations.

In Baton Rouge, a team of CNN engineers has already found a riverfront location on a pier. There's a big building several hundred yards away that can protect the satellite truck. As long as the satellite dish works, you can broadcast, so keeping it safe is essential. The problem is, the dish acts as a sail. It can get picked up by a strong wind, causing the truck it's attached to to flip over. You have to find a spot where the satellite truck is protected by a building on at least two sides. That way even when the hurricane winds shift, the dish will not be directly hit.

After covering several hurricanes, you start to know what to expect. At first the winds just pick up gently. Then it starts to rain. Your fancy Gore-Tex clothing keeps you dry for about thirty minutes; then the water starts to seep in. Within an hour you're completely wet. Your feet slosh around in your boots, and your hands are wrinkled and white. If you've ever wondered what your skin will look like when you're eighty-five, try standing in a hurricane for a few hours.

Katrina comes ashore at 6:10 A.M., on Monday near Buras, Louisiana. The sustained winds are estimated to be 125 miles per hour, a category 3 hurricane. In Baton Rouge, conditions deteriorate rapidly. What seemed like high winds just a few hours ago now seem calm by comparison. The electricity goes out, transformers explode, lighting up the darkened sky with greenish blue flares. I can't see any debris flying through the air; I can only hear it: the snap of tree branches, the twisting of signs, aluminum roofs ripping loose. You can't tell where the noise is coming from or where the debris is headed.

Between live shots I sit inside my SUV, dripping in steamy darkness. As the storm intensifies, other reporters' transmissions get knocked off the air, so the network starts coming back to me more and more—live shot after live shot. Chris Davis, my cameraman, can barely see through his viewfinder, but he keeps working, steadying himself against the railing of the pier. After a while I'm just repeating myself: "It's really blowing now… and the rain, it's torrential." There's really not much else to say. It's water and it's wind. How many ways are there to describe them?

You see weird stuff in a storm: floating Coke machines, boats washed up on roads. During Hurricane Frances, two guys in a brand-new Humvee with HURRICANE RESEARCH TEAM printed on the

side pulled into the marina where we were working. From their matching yellow raincoats, I assumed they were scientists, but it turned out they were just two guys with a storm fetish. I last saw them around 1:00 A.M. They were hooting and hollering and videotaping each other getting tossed around by 110-mile-per-hour gusts of wind.

It's easy to get caught up in all the excitement, easy to forget that while you are talking on TV, someone is cowering in a closet with their kids, or drowning in their own living room.

After Hurricane Charley, I drove around Punta Gorda, Florida, surveying the damage. There was aluminum siding wrapped around trees, shockingly silver in the morning sun; a family's photo album lay in the street; a sofa sat on top of a car. A relief official mistakenly said that there were a dozen or more bodies at one trailer park, and all the morning-show reporters in mobile news vans crisscrossed the small town searching for the dead. They'd slow down and ask local residents if they knew of a nearby trailer park where "something" had happened. (No one wanted to come right out and ask, "Seen any dead people around here?")

In the end, the real power of a hurricane isn't found in its wind speed. It's in what it leaves behind—the lives lost, the lives changed, the memories obliterated in a gust of wind. Anyone who does hurricane reporting for any length of time knows all too well that standing in the aftermath of a storm is much more difficult than standing in the storm itself, no matter how hard the winds blow.

At the height of Katrina, I'm holding on to the railing of a pier, surrounded by a whirling wall of white. Between live shots, my arms stretch out, my eyes close, I don't care if anyone sees. The storm is a phantom, rearing, retreating, charging. It spins and slaps, pirouettes and punishes. I'm submerged in water, corseted by the air. I lean my shoulders into the wind, spread my legs so I don't fall when the gust weakens. If I shift the wrong way, it will take me. I could just let it. I've felt the tug. A few more steps and I'd be gone. Crushed by the wall of water and wind. It's that close. I can feel it.

It sounds a little crazy, perhaps, but you do get caught up in the challenge, trying to stay on air, trying to get as close as you can. During Hurricane Ivan, in 2004, I kept insisting on staying out longer and longer. We were on a balcony in Mobile, Alabama, a perfect spot to witness the storm. At one point, my producers tied a rope around my leg so they could pull me back if I got knocked

down. Finally, they insisted we move inside. I reluctantly agreed.

In Baton Rouge, for a while I can't see the camera lens because of the rain. It doesn't really matter, though; I know what I'm supposed to say: "I am powerless in the face of the storm." That's what reporters always say. "The storm's a reminder of how weak we humans really are." Right now, however, at this moment, I don't feel any of that. I feel invincible. The storm whips around me, flows through me. I am able to work, to stand, even when it's at its worst. The satellite dish is up, we are on the air, we're just about the only ones left. We have beaten the elements. We have won.

By noon the worst of it is over. Katrina is moving on, heading toward Mississippi. I want nothing more to do with it. That's the way it always is. The wind weakens, the adrenaline wanes, and my body shuts down. Face scrubbed raw, whipped for hours by the elements, eyes itching, I long for sleep, but have to stay up, look for survivors, locate the dead. We do a quick reconnaissance around Baton

Rouge and see that the damage is limited. There's no word on when the road into New Orleans will reopen, and I have to be on the air again in seven hours, so my producer, John Murgatroyd, and I decide to follow the storm as it heads east. We want to catch the tail end of it.

We leave the satellite truck, and head to Meridian, Mississippi, where we think the storm is going. We're told that another satellite truck will meet us there. Wet, tired, we pile into the SUV, drive east, then north, constantly buffeted by dangerously high winds. The speedometer says we're going a hundred miles per hour. I try not to check it all that much; we have to beat the storm.

Near Jackson, trees are down, roads are flooded. It's raining so hard we can barely see where we are. We finally find the satellite truck, by a boarded-up gas station on the outskirts of Meridian. It's not an ideal spot from which to broadcast, but we have no choice. We're expected to go live in half an hour. It takes about twenty minutes for the engineer to set up, and when we finally connect to New York on the satellite, I can hear people in the control room nervously yelling, checking our audio levels, trying to fix some problems with the picture we are sending them. The minutes tick by.

With thirty seconds to go, we're still trying to make sure our transmission is working. Ten seconds before airtime I'm told we're good to go.

We stay on the air for several hours, during which Katrina is downgraded to a tropical storm. By 10:00 P.M. we're done. We're almost out of fuel, but luckily CNN has gotten us reservations in nearby Philadelphia, Mississippi. Amazingly, a casino run by Choctaw Indians is still open for business.

During big storms most hotels shut their doors. Casinos, however, always try to stay open. They'll do whatever it takes to keep the slots running and the cash coming in. When we arrive, a few elderly ladies, blue tint–washed hair, sit at the slots, pulling the levers, their eyes fixed on the flashing lights. When I get into my room, the smell of mildew is overwhelming. The window is broken; it must have happened during the storm. Water is running down the wall, spreading onto the carpet like a bloodstain. My eyes ache, my feet throb. Sleep is close; it's just on the other side of my eyelids. All I have to do is lie down. Breathe. Close my eyes.

My father didn't like gambling, at least as a teenager. I know this because when he was sixteen he wrote a letter to the **Meridian Star** about gambling's negative effects. I found a copy of the newspaper recently, in a scrapbook he kept as a kid. It was sitting in storage, in a box of his papers I'd never gone through.

"Many a person who has strayed from the straight and narrow way began his erring at some slot machine dive," he wrote. I laughed when I read the letter. It sounded so priggish, his teenage voice so unlike the open-minded man I remember.

Quitman, Mississippi, where he was born, is just a few miles south of Meridian. During World War II his family moved to New Orleans, but they didn't stay there for long. When they came back to Mississippi, they settled in Meridian. My grandmother opened a general store, and my father worked as an announcer at the local radio station while taking classes at the junior college.

I was eight when my father took my brother and me to Mississippi to see where he was born. We drove out to Quitman, to where their house had been, but found no sign of it, just some faded bricks where the chimney once stood. He'd grown up in a small wooden house on some 250 acres of farm and pasture land. The barns were gone as well, the wood long since rotted. The pasture, the peach orchard, the cotton fields had been reclaimed by trees and underbrush, buried under canyons of kudzu.

We'd walked around Quitman, stopping in at stores, running into old friends my father had gone to school with.

My father's name was Wyatt, but in Mississippi, when he was a boy, everybody called him Buddy.

"Buddy, that boy is the spitting image of you," people said when they stopped to talk to us during that visit. It made me happy to hear, though at the time I didn't see the resemblance. Now I look at pictures of myself and I see my father's face.

Tuesday. I wake up hungover, not sure where I am or what's happened. Cellphone, TV, BlackBerry— I check them all, but nothing works. I've no idea what the storm has done. Outside, the wind still whips. Light rain. A line of police cruisers snakes through the hotel's parking lot. I'm sick of this. Yesterday I told myself I was going to quit covering hurricanes for a while. No more. Then the winds bumped up, and my heart quickened once again.

I stumble out of bed and walk downstairs to the parking lot, where the satellite engineer is checking on his truck. There's a phone on board that works as long as the truck has gas. For the next few days this will be the only phone communication we have with the world beyond.

When I finally get a call through to the assignment desk at CNN in Atlanta, they don't have a lot of detailed information.

"We know it's bad," the supervising producer tells me. "We don't know how bad. We've seen pictures out of Gulfport, and it appears heavily damaged."

In New Orleans the levees have already failed. The city is flooding. Eventually 80 percent of it will be underwater. The Superdome is already overcrowded; the air-conditioning system has broken down. As the floodwaters rise, thousands more will seek shelter at the Convention Center, where they will find no medical care, no food, no way out.

We decide to head to Gulfport. At least we'll be near the water, and depending on what we find, we can figure out where to go next. The problem is gas. We don't have enough. The electricity is out in much of Philadelphia. I hear that the nearby Wal-Mart is open, and when we get there I'm surprised to see that their gas pumps still work. We fill up our vehicles, and buy as much food and water as we can find. Waiting in line to pay, a woman recognizes me and suggests we go to Bay St. Louis, a small coastal community west of Gulfport. She's a teacher and thinks her school may have been destroyed.

"We can't get any word out of there," she tells me. "They're not saying anything about it on the radio. No one ever talks about the little towns."

Back in the parking lot, we convene our small band. We have two camera crews, three SUVs, and a satellite truck. The main roads south are closed, but we hear on the radio that one highway is open for emergency vehicles only. We figure we're eligible, and move out.

We drive past downed trees and power lines; debris litters the highway. Miles of scattered steel and broken homes. I see the misery, but I keep on going. After a while it becomes just a blur. It's a strange sensation, a schizophrenic feeling. People have died, but we are alive. Others are stuck; we are moving forward. We have gas and food, a phone. We can raise our satellite dish and broadcast around the world; all it takes is a few minutes to set up.

I don't know where I'm going exactly, but I know what I'll do when I get there. There are pictures to take, a story to tell. All the rest falls away. Right now I have no bills, no mortgage, no mundane details of life to worry about—just this moment, this mission. I've been here before, sat in this seat, looked out this window at a hundred different landscapes passing by—Sri Lanka, Niger, Somalia, Bosnia. This moment, this feeling exists only at the edge of the world. It never lasts long, like a rare orchid that grows only in treacherous terrain.

When we get to Gulfport, the motion stops and reality sets in. It's worse than I imagined. The worst I've ever seen in America. Sri Lanka after the tsunami is the closest comparison I can make. For a moment that's where I think I am: Kamburugamuwa. Little Maduranga throwing stones at the sea.

Downtown Gulfport is in shambles. People

stagger about with no shoes, licking at their tears. Tractor trailer trucks that have been flung about, lie in a pile like abandoned children's toys. Nearby, a seal lies stunned, alive, barking in an asphalt parking lot. A lady douses it with cups of water, trying to keep the seal alive. When she leaves, police shoot it in the head. Two bullets. Point blank. I remember being surprised the scarlet blood didn't spread very far.

Next to the waterfront, a casino barge, a block long, sits on dry land. Through a gash in the side, silver slot machines sparkle. An urban search-and-rescue team walks by in the dying light in steel-toe boots, with lamps on their helmets, looking for anyone who may be alive. "Hello!" they call out. "Hello!" Silence.

———

Wednesday morning we're in Waveland, Mississippi. We drove from Gulfport in the first light of day. Coast Guard helicopters pass overhead on their way to New Orleans to pluck people off rooftops, and bring in badly needed supplies. Choppers from all over the region are heading there.

Nobody seems to land here. I've heard only a few reports out of Louisiana. We still have no cell phones, no e-mail. I know the levees have broken, and so have the promises. The city is flooded. It was predicted, but no one seems prepared. The Superdome, the Convention Center, the places people were told to go, are overwhelmed.

Mississippi has no levees, no wide-scale looting. Here the drama is of a wholly different sort. The water has pulled back into the Gulf of Mexico, leaving the land dry, destroyed. On every block, around every corner, there is loss. In Bay St. Louis and Waveland, miles of shore-front homes are gone. Block after block, nothing but debris. I'm not shocked by the loss of property; it's staggering, but destruction is nothing new. It's the silence that shocks me. There's no heavy earth-moving equipment, no trucks with aid rumbling past. I stand in a field of timber that once was a street and can hear the wind blowing through the remains of people's lives. A sheet of plastic caught in a tree rustles in the breeze. Flies swarm over the corpse of a dog. A helicopter moves on the horizon. It intrudes, for a few seconds, then silence once again.

I spot a team of men picking through the rubble. They're part of an urban search-and-rescue

task force from Virginia. One man carries a small video camera attached to a metal pole. He uses it to check beneath piles of debris to see if anyone is trapped. They've been down this street before, but a local woman has said that someone is still missing from here, so they're searching again.

The pavement is completely covered with crushed roofs of homes. One of the searchers, Scott Prentice, carefully makes his way amid the debris. His progress is slow, steady.

"We can't search all of these with all these boards," he says, stepping over a marine's dress jacket lying in the rubble. A child's naked doll hangs from a tree; its eyelids close and open. "We could spend weeks right here," Prentice says, shaking his head, "but we have to move on." He breathes deeply, seeing if he can catch the smell of a corpse.

The Virginia task force has set up a base camp nearby, in the parking lot of a Rite Aid pharmacy. When we get there, a woman named Sally Slaughter stops by to report a missing person. Slaughter is small and thin. Her worn face is hidden beneath a baseball cap. She works in a nearby motel and is worried that her co-worker Christina Bane is dead.

"I went with some other neighbors to her house

this morning, and it was still boarded up," Slaughter tells one of the searchers. "We broke open a back window and there was a body right there in the kitchen."

Slaughter knew that Christina Bane and her family didn't evacuate. "They were scared of leaving their house 'cause of looters," she tells me. Later, I learn the real reason they'd stayed: Bane's two sons were disabled, and she didn't want to go to a shelter where people would stare.

"I don't want to say they were retarded, exactly," Slaughter says, "but they were a little slow."

Anytime a corpse is found, the Virginia task force's body identification unit has to photograph it, and mark its location for recovery. Right now, there are no places to take the bodies; the local morgues are flooded, and so are the private funeral homes. Eventually FEMA will send in refrigerated trucks to store the dead, but it will take several days for the first ones to arrive.

At the Banes' house, Sally points to the window she broke open earlier this morning. The house is still. I can smell the bodies. Holding my breath, I press my face up to the rear window, dirty with mud. It takes a few seconds for me to realize what I'm looking at. There's a man lying in front of me. He's covered in mud and sediment, trapped amid

piles of lumber and insulation. I assume it's Edgar Bane, Christina's husband. He's badly bloated, twisted and swollen like a birthday balloon about to pop. One of his arms is stuck at a right angle. Rigor mortis has set in.

He's the first storm fatality I've come across so far. I've seen drowning victims before—in Sri Lanka and elsewhere—but never here in America. I didn't expect it to make a difference, but it does.

The front door is jammed, blocked by pieces of debris left behind when the water receded. The team begins prying open a window. It doesn't take them long. As soon as the window opens, the odor pours out. Everyone has to stand back.

Christina Bane is inside. So are Edgar and their two sons, Carl and Edgar Junior. All four are dead. Drowned. Sally Slaughter is crying. She's the only one. One of the searchers takes out a camera—digital, downloadable—and shoots pictures of the Banes. Click. Click. Click. Click. Another searcher takes out a Magic Marker. On the Banes' front door he writes **V** for victims. 4 DEAD.

A few blocks from the Banes' home, the searchers find a body lying on a sidewalk in an empty cul-de-sac. I think it's a woman; at first, it's hard to tell. Water wipes away identity, race, even gender. I think she's African American, but her skin appears white, translucent almost.

Someone has covered her face and part of her body with a dirty bedspread. Her feet and hands stick out.

"Did she drown here?" I ask one of the searchers.

"No," he tells me. "Apparently, she died in one of these buildings here. The residents kind of dumped her here. This has become the dumping ground for people that have died."

The team takes pictures—Click. Click—then records the woman's GPS coordinates. Later they'll mark the spot on a map. It's dotted with small circles for each of the bodies they've found so far.

"Do you ever get used to this?" I ask David Cash, the team's doctor.

"Hurricane Ivan, Opal, the Pentagon, Oklahoma City," he says, listing some of the disasters he's worked on in the last eleven years. "You never get used to it; it just needs to be done."

I ask Chris Davis, my cameraman, to take some

tight shots of the woman's hand and one of her feet. The image of her body, covered in the bedspread, will be too grisly for television, but I don't want to ignore the reality of what's happened here. Dr. Cash and his team climb back in their vehicle. We get back in ours, and follow them out.

I never thought I'd see this here, in America—the dead left out like trash. None of us speaks. There's nothing you can say.

Chris is having a hard time with the bodies. I see it in his face. At first, I don't understand what the problem is. Then I realize it's his first time.

My father's corpse was the first one I ever saw. His wake was at the Frank E. Campbell Funeral Chapel in New York. I passed the building for years on my way to school and never knew what went on inside.

I didn't recognize him at first. I hadn't known how different the dead really look—the sickening stillness, the flatness of an embalmed face. He resembled a figure cut from some soft stone.

I remember the clothes my father wore in the casket, the unnatural way they lay on his body. Already I felt his absence, missed his embrace, the comfort of having him near. At night we'd watch TV. He'd stretch out on the floor on his back, his head perched on a pillow. I'd lay perpendicular to him, my head resting on the soft part of his stomach, which rose and fell with each breath.

My father was born a Baptist but had long since moved away from the fire-and-brimstone preachers of his youth. He no longer went to services, and his funeral was held in a Unitarian church.

"When you mark 'Unitarian' down in the hospital," I remember him saying, "they don't know what it means, so they don't send any minister to bother you."

After the funeral, I stood in a receiving line with my mother and brother. People I didn't know filed past, shaking my hand. Later, there was a gathering at our apartment. A few friends from school. A teacher I particularly liked.

My nanny, May, who'd helped raise me since I was born, had just returned from a trip home to her native Scotland. She rushed back when she learned of my father's death.

"Don't worry, May. Everything will be okay," I told her. Years later she cried as she recounted the moment. "Of course, it wasn't okay," she said. "Nothing was ever okay again."

———

It's Wednesday, August 31, 2005. I'm still in Waveland, Mississippi, reporting on Katrina's aftermath. Women sob searching for family photographs. Middle-age men beg to use my satellite phone. Every conversation starts the same: "Mom, it's me. I'm alive."

I see the president's plane fly over Mississippi.

"Do you think he can see the corpses from so high up?" a resident asks me as we watch the jet streak by.

It's more than forty-eight hours after the storm, and there's still no one to pick up the dead. It's unconscionable. Soldiers have a motto: "Leave no man behind." I saw it stenciled on a blast wall on an army base outside Baghdad. They'll risk life and limb to recover the body of a fellow soldier. Many have died over the years doing just that. There are front lines in America as well, and right now Waveland is one of them. These people should not be left to rot.

As dusk falls, I go back to the site where the dead woman was lying. She is still there. I think about trying to move her, but I have no equipment, no gloves, and besides, there's nowhere to put her. I feel powerless, weak.

For the last two nights, I've been a guest on **Larry King Live,** and listened as politicians thanked one another for the "Herculean" efforts they were undertaking in the wake of this "unprecedented" and "unpredictable" disaster. I don't know what they're talking about. I see their lips move, I hear the sounds, but it doesn't make any sense.

"Stop thanking each other" I want to yell. "Grab a body bag and get down here with some soldiers!" Instead I nod and listen. Night after night.

Wednesday, I interview FEMA director Michael Brown. I tell him I'm not seeing much of a response here, and there are bodies lying in the street. It's "unacceptable," he says. He promises he's "working on it." After the program, someone from FEMA tells my producer we can follow Brown around the next day. Later, however, they call back and rescind the offer.

Politicians keep saying that they know people are "frustrated." If they really understood, however, they wouldn't use that word. **Frustrated** is waiting on line for a film; it's a slow-moving train. The feelings here go much deeper. People aren't "frustrated." They are dead. They are dying; the scales have fallen from their eyes. I remember what Dr. Tectonidis told me in Niger, about the mothers in the intensive care ward. "They don't want your sympathy," he said, "they want you to do your job."

In normal times you can't always say what's right and what's wrong. The truth is not always clear. Here, however, all the doubt is stripped away. This isn't about Republicans and Democrats, theories and politics. Relief is either here or it's not. Corpses don't lie.

When you're working, you're focused on getting the shot, writing the story. You sometimes don't notice how upset you are. In Waveland, I certainly don't. Late Wednesday night, I'm talking to someone back in the office about the woman we left on the street, and I find myself crying. I can't even speak. I have to call that person back. At first I don't realize what's happening to me. It's been years since a story made me cry. Sarajevo was probably the last time. I've never been on this kind of story, though, in my own country. It's something I never expected to see.

I used to get back from Somalia or Sarajevo and

imagine what New York would look like in a war. Which buildings would crumble? Who among my friends would survive? I always told myself if it did happen here, at least we could handle it better. At least our government would know what to do.

In Sri Lanka, in Niger, you never assume anyone will help. You take it for granted that governments don't work, that people are on their own. There's a different level of expectation. Here, you grow up believing there's a safety net, that things can never completely fall apart. Katrina showed us all that's not true. For all the money spent on homeland security, all the preparations that have allegedly been made, we are not ready, not even for a disaster we know is coming. We can't take care of our own. The world can break apart in our own backyard, and when it does many of us will simply fall off.

Thursday. I'm about to interview Senator Mary Landrieu. She's a Democrat from Louisiana. I'm unaware she's going to be on the program until a few minutes before she appears. Much of what we're doing on the air each night is impromptu. I like working that way best. No scripts, no Tele-PrompTer, just talking with the viewers—no separation between me and the camera. Before I go on air each night, I have a rough idea what will be in the program: where our reporters are located and what they've been working on. During the broadcast, however, much of that changes, so I have to be quick on my feet, ready for anything.

As a child, I used to spend summers at the beach, and I loved to run along the edge of the sand cliffs made by the retreating tide. As I ran, I could feel the sand collapse beneath me, but as long as I kept moving forward, kept running fast, I could stay one step ahead of the falling cliff. That's what anchoring the news is like. You can easily falter, easily destroy your career in a sentence or two. The key is to keep going, keep moving, never forget you're running on sand.

I'm standing in a small clearing in a field of destroyed homes. It used to be someone's front yard. Senator Landrieu is in Baton Rouge. I can't see her; I can only hear her through my plastic earpiece.

I start by asking her if the federal government bears responsibility for what is happening. "Should they apologize for what is happening now?" I ask.

"Anderson, there will be plenty of time to discuss all of those issues, about why, and how, and what, and if," Landrieu says. "But, Anderson, as you understand, and all of the producers and directors of CNN, and the news networks, this situation is very serious and it's going to demand all of our full attention through the hours, through the nights, through the days.

"Let me just say a few things. Thank President Clinton and former President Bush for their strong statements of support and comfort today. I thank all the leaders that are coming to Louisiana, and Mississippi, and Alabama to our help and rescue.

"We are grateful for the military assets that are being brought to bear. I want to thank Senator Frist and Senator Reid for their extraordinary efforts.

"Anderson, tonight, I don't know if you've heard—maybe you all have announced it—but Congress is going to an unprecedented session to pass a ten-billion-dollar supplemental bill tonight to keep FEMA and the Red Cross up and operating."

I can't believe she is thanking people. In Waveland, the bodies haven't been picked up; the National Guard is just starting to arrive. In New Orleans, no help has come to the Convention

Center; the Superdome is unbearable for those still stuck there. I literally cannot believe what she is saying.

"Excuse me, Senator. I'm sorry for interrupting," I say. "I haven't heard that, because for the last four days I've been seeing dead bodies in the streets here in Mississippi. And to listen to politicians thanking each other and complimenting each other—you know, I've got to tell you, there are a lot of people here who are very upset, and very angry, and very frustrated.

"And when they hear politicians slap—you know, thanking one another, it just, you know, it kind of cuts them the wrong way right now, because literally there was a body on the streets of this town yesterday being eaten by rats because this woman had been lying in the street for forty-eight hours. And there's not enough facilities to take her up. Do you get the anger that is out here?"

"Anderson, I have the anger inside of me," she responds. "Most of the homes in my family have been destroyed. Our homes have been destroyed. I understand what you're saying, and I know all of those details. And the president of the United States knows those details."

"Well, who are you angry at?" I ask her.

"I'm not angry at anyone," she says. "I'm just

expressing that it is so important for everyone in this nation to pull together, for all military assets and all assets to be brought to bear in this situation. And I have every confidence that this country is as great and as strong as we can be to do that. And that effort is under way."

"Well, I mean, there are a lot of people here who are kind of ashamed of what is happening in this country right now," I say. "Ashamed of what is happening in your state, certainly, and that's not to blame the people who are there. It's a desperate situation. But...no one seems to be taking responsibility. I mean, I know you say there's a time and a place for...looking back, but this seems to be the time and the place. I mean, there are people who want answers, and there are people who want someone to stand up and say, 'You know what? We should have done more.' Are all the assets being brought to bear? I mean, today, for the first time, I'm seeing National Guard troops in this town."

"Anderson, I know," she says. "And I know where you are. And I know what you're seeing. Believe me, we know it. And we understand, and there will be a time to talk about all of that. Trust me. I know what the people are suffering. The governor knows. The president knows. The military officials know. And they're trying to do the very best they can to stabilize the situation. Senator Vitter, our congressional delegation, all of us understand what is happening. We are doing our very, very best to get the situation under control. But I want to thank the president. He will be here tomorrow, we think. And the military is sending assets as we speak.

"So, please, I understand. You might say I'm a politician, but I grew up in New Orleans. My father was the mayor of that city. I've represented that city my whole life, and it's just not New Orleans. It's St. Bernard, and St. Tammany, and Plaquemines Parish that have been completely underwater. Our levee system has failed. We need a lot of help. And the Congress has been wonderful to help us, and we need more help. Nobody's perfect, Anderson. Everybody has to stand up here. And I know you understand. So thank you so much for everything you're doing."

When it's done, there is silence in my ear. We are in a commercial break, and my producers are not saying a thing. I worry I've crossed the line. I hate TV anchors who are rude, and I never want to be disrespectful to any guest on my program. I always pride myself on not wearing my opinion on my sleeve, and on being able to adapt to a given situation and discuss ideas with anyone. This is different, though. No one has any information, and people are desperate. The least our politicians can do is answer questions. It seems to me totally inappropriate to stick to sound-bite statements and praise of the president.

Three days later, Senator Landrieu appears on **ABC News,** being interviewed by George Stephanopoulos. Her tone seems to have changed. She says she is upset about the pace of relief efforts and angry about federal criticism of New Orleans police. "If one person criticizes our sheriffs," Landrieu says, "or says one more thing, including the President of the United States, he will hear from me—one more word about it...and I might likely have to punch him—literally."

Just as we come back from commercial break, a pickup truck drives by. In the back a young man with a trucker hat holds up a tattered American flag. He salvaged it from the wreckage. He's tired and worn, but proud of that flag, proud that he and his family are still standing. We don't speak— he is too far away—but I look him in the eye and we nod to each other. In his face I think I detect betrayal and anger, but also strength and resolve. I'm on the air, but I find myself tearing up. My throat tightens; I'm almost unable to speak. I quickly try to move on to another story, and hope no one has noticed.

———

My dad used to cry often: in movies, at church, once even in a restaurant in Mobile. A woman moved among the tables singing "Amazing Grace," and tears rolled down his cheeks. I always found it embarrassing. When he was a child, a relative whom everyone called Mr. Raspberry was known for his prodigious crying. Mr. Raspberry was a devout Pentacostalist, and one year at a family reunion he became overcome with emotion. Weeping, he shouted, "Glory to God! We've all been spared another year!"

"Why does Mr. Raspberry cry so much?" my father asked his grandmother.

"Oh, if you ask me, his bladder's just located too close to his eyes," she said.

There is so much about my father I'm just starting to remember, so much I recognize now that I'm nearing the same age he was when I was born. My father wrote a book called **Families,** a memoir about growing up in Mississippi. The book is a celebration of family and of the importance of re-membering one's roots. He wrote it two years be-fore he died, as a letter to my brother and me. I think he knew he wouldn't live to see us grow into men. His father had died young, and his sister El-sie had died of a heart attack when she was just thirty-eight. I know he worried that in his absence my brother and I would forget our Mississippi roots, our blood connection to the South.

When my father's book came out, he went on speaking tours throughout Mississippi and several times brought my brother and me along. He didn't try to hide the state's faults from us. He'd been an early champion of civil rights and made sure we were aware of Mississippi's history of racial injus-tice. Meridian was the hometown of James Cheney, the civil rights worker killed in Philadelphia, Mis-sissippi, by local Klansmen. My father told us all about Cheney and the civil rights movement in the South. He saw the good and bad in his home state, and his love of Mississippi was richer for it.

Growing up in New York, we were always aware of my mother's family's history. It was hard not to be. We lived for a time not far from Vanderbilt Av-enue, and Grand Central Station, where there is an imposing statue of my great-great-great-grandfather, Cornelius Vanderbilt, the founder of the New York Central Railroad. After seeing it for the first time when I was six, I became convinced that everyone's grandparents turned into statues when they died.

My father's family may have been poor, but they had branches of aristocracy as well. Men who weren't rich, but who carried themselves regally. My great-granduncle Jim Bull fought at Chicka-mauga, one of the bloodiest battles of the Civil War. It was said he never got over the habit of kill-ing, and once shot a man for cussing in front of a group of women. According to my grandfather, "he never killed nobody that didn't deserve it." He died trapped under an overturned train. Ac-cording to family legend, when the steam began to scald him, he attempted to cut off his legs with a pocketknife.

My great-grandfather William Preston Cooper also lived by his own set of rules. He had a num-ber of illegitimate children , and on his deathbed, at the age of eighty-four, he shouted to horrified family members that if they'd just "bring a woman to my bed, I'd have no need of dying."

After my father's death, our trips to Mississippi all but stopped. For a few summers my brother and I went for weekend visits to stay with family friends. We'd see our relatives for just a few hours— strained meetings that always made me sad.

For years after he died, I used to imagine that my father would somehow give me a sign, sometimes I still search for it, his approval, his advice. Friends of his tell me, "Your father would have been so proud of you," but it's not the same as hearing it from him, seeing it in his face. I like to think of him watching my show each night. I like to imagine he's seeing it all.

"God bless you. You have no idea how happy we are to have you here," a man says to me Friday morning, shaking my hand in a rubble-strewn lot in Waveland. His name is Charles Kearney, and he and his wife, Germaine, have come to visit what's left of their home.

"Where are the people?" Charles shouts. "Why are people dying? I'll tell you why! Because there aren't enough National Guard troops to come here! They're all already dispersed! I mean, I hate to go there, but why else can it be? They're in Iraq and everywhere else."

"Foreign countries are getting better care than we get," Germaine says.

Charles and Germaine lost their house on Honey Ridge Road. So have their parents, who lived a few blocks away.

They evacuated on Sunday to Mobile. They've been coming back each day, ferrying food and water to friends from their hotel.

"I'm speechless. What the hell is going on and why are people still on the freaking interstate in New Orleans?" Charles says, his face turning red with anger. "I don't care whose fault it is, but fix it now. And these people who are saying, 'You know, well we tried! We warned them. They could get out!' Well people don't have the resources to get out. They have nowhere to go."

Charles and Germaine take me to where Charles's parents' house used to stand. His mother and father, Myrtle and Bill Kearney, are picking up plates from their yard.

"Oh goodness, Anderson, I don't want to look like transient trash," Myrtle says, laughing when she sees me. "This house was so pretty. My father-in-law built it painstakingly. He would come to the lot, he would study the best views to put the windows."

"Look, our whole kitchen counter's over there," Germaine says, pointing.

Myrtle is holding a cracked plate in her hand.

"What are you going to do with that?" I ask.

"Probably frame it," she says, laughing. "For God's sake, I'm an artist! I'll probably paint it."

Myrtle didn't want to evacuate at first, but on Sunday, Charles convinced her she had to go.

"I vacuumed my house to the moon before we left to go for the hurricane," she says, shaking her head. "I cleaned the house so that when we came back we would have a pleasant environment to come back in."

"We stood right here in this driveway and laughed at her as we left," Charles says.

"And wait," she adds. "You wanna hear the best? Y'all are gonna die laughing. I collect rocks. I came out, picked out all my rocks and brought 'em inside and hid 'em! The rocks are gone. And the carpet's gone! And it's gonna be so damned easy to move, you won't believe it!"

I laugh with Myrtle, and realize it's the first time in days. Later, however, away from her family, her laughter is gone, her smiling face falls away.

"There's nothing that can prepare you for this,"

she says. "I have not cried yet. And I'm probably gonna go away and lose it completely. With all my joking and all my Myrtle-isms, I'm probably gonna lose it really bad. But right now...what can you say?...And this is the God's truth for me: we have each other, right here. Some people don't, and some people don't have water to drink right now. And some people have dialysis and they need drugs. We can't complain about this. This happens to other people, and they come back from it. And we're going to come back from it, too."

The next day, Saturday, I leave for New Orleans. It's only about fifty miles from Waveland, but the drive takes several hours because of roadblocks and traffic. Our team has grown over the last few days, and when we line up to convoy to Louisiana we have at least fifteen vehicles. CNN has sent trucks from Atlanta with food and gas so we can operate independently for weeks. They've also sent two RVs so we'll have a place to sleep.

New Orleans is largely underwater. The evacuation of the Superdome has just been completed.

After days of waiting and inexplicable delays, buses arrived to take the stranded to Houston's Astrodome. The Convention Center has just started being evacuated. Medical tents have been set up across the street, and helicopters land nearby to shuttle the most vulnerable evacuees to the airport and shelters in Baton Rouge. Coast Guard helicopters continue to fly over the city, occasionally hovering over flooded neighborhoods to pick up people still stranded in their homes.

CNN has set up a base at the New Orleans airport, and we briefly stop there to pick up some gear—waders and handheld satellite phones. When we enter the city, it feels like we're crossing a frontier. The farther we go the more we find stripped away. Maps are useless. We double-back from dead ends and slowly find our way along the water's edge. We head toward the Lower Ninth Ward.

A few blocks from Bourbon Street, we stop at a police station to borrow a boat. A cowboy crew of cops has been holed up there for days. A hand-drawn sign on a sheet of cardboard hangs over the entrance. FORT APACHE, it says. That's what they've renamed the station.

"We call it Fort Apache 'cause we're surrounded by water and Indians," says a cop with a cowboy hat and swimming goggles around his neck.

"Why are you wearing swimming goggles?" I ask.

"Because if things get really hot, I'm just going to swim out of here." I can't tell if he's serious or not. I don't think he knows, either.

I feel like a character in a Joseph Conrad novel. I've turned the bend in the river and found an isolated tribe armed to the teeth. They've been out on their own too long and are dazed by the horror.

"We're survivors, man. We're survivors," a young African American cop tells me, clutching a shotgun. He's talking to me but stares far away. "It's a war zone, man, but we're alive. The criminal element tried to get us down but they couldn't get us. We stayed together. They thought they could get us, but they can't. That's how it's going down."

He graduated from the police academy just four weeks ago. "Nothing they showed us in the academy could have prepared us for this," he says, slowly shaking his head, "but you gotta do what you gotta do."

Tricked out like a storm scavenger, one cop wears a Kukri tucked in his belt. It's a thick knife with a curved blade, used by Gurkhas in Nepal. I had one when I was a kid. It's said that a Gurkha can split a man from his collar bone to his waist with one slice of a Kukri. I don't ask this guy if he's ever used it.

The police say they've been taking incoming fire the last couple of nights. Now they've posted snipers on the roofs of surrounding buildings. "Shoot to kill, man. Shoot to kill," one cop says, smiling.

They loan us their boat so we can go out into the Lower Ninth Ward. Actually, it's CNN's boat. Chris Lawrence, a reporter for CNN, brought it into New Orleans the day after Katrina and loaned it to these cops so they could rescue their families and others.

"Shouldn't the city have had some boats ready for you guys to use?" I ask one of the sergeants.

He just stares at me.

"Don't get me started on the list of things this city should have done," another cop says, spitting. "You'd think they would preposition some vehicles or some extra ammunition or guns, but they didn't. There was no go-to point if disaster happens, no word on what to do. Nothing was in place. Nothing."

The French Quarter wasn't flooded, but it's a short drive from it to the water's edge. We climb into a pickup full of police, all of us huddled in the back. Guns stick out from all directions. It's the first time these police officers have been out on patrol. We drive down St. Claude Avenue, strangers in a strange land. A few residents glance at us as we pass. They move slowly, still shell-shocked by the storm. Some carry gallon jugs of water. They're searching for food. I squint, and for a second I'm back in Somalia, riding in a pickup with a half-dozen gunmen. No rules, no future, no past. Only this moment, this feeling. It's gone as soon as I think of it.

"Watch the windows at the school," one of the cops says, and they all spin around, pointing their guns at a large three-story building we're passing on our right.

"That's Frederick Douglass," one of the officers explains. "It's been taken over." He doesn't say by whom, but he's clearly nervous, unsure what kind of reception we might receive in this neighborhood.

Many of the windows in the school are broken,

and the front doors are wide open. At the top of the building, carved into the façade it reads, FRANCIS T. NICHOLLS PUBLIC HIGH SCHOOL. The name sounds familiar, though I can't place it at first. Once we're about a block away, I remember: My father graduated from high school in New Orleans. Francis T. Nicholls was his old school.

My father's family moved to New Orleans in 1943. He was sixteen years old. His mother came because there were jobs in the city and because her two married daughters had already moved here with their husbands. My father lived with his mother and five of his seven siblings in a ground-floor apartment in the Ninth Ward, a few blocks from Francis T. Nicholls High School.

My grandmother got a job at Higgens-Hughes, a plant that manufactured boats for the war effort. My grandfather didn't like New Orleans, and had stayed in Mississippi, trying to keep the farm going. He couldn't find workers, though, because so many men had left to fight or to labor in factories. When he finally decided he couldn't keep the farm running, he leased the land and got a job as a fireman for the Mississippi railroad.

My father fell in love with New Orleans from the start. It seemed to him a foreign and mysterious city. He saw his first opera in New Orleans and his first ballet as well. Compared with Quitman, it was like living on another planet.

He graduated from Francis T. Nicholls in 1944. In his scrapbook, I found a clipping from a New Orleans paper describing the graduation ceremony.

Next to the article, my father had pasted a picture of his senior class. The school was segregated then. In the photo, the boys all wear ties and vests, the girls knee-length dresses. My father stands off to the side, a smile on his face. He drew an arrow above his head, and wrote ME on the side of the page.

It made me smile. When I was five I'd done the same thing. My parents threw a party for Charlie Chaplin when he returned for the first time to the United States after living in Switzerland for some twenty years. I was photographed shaking his hand, and the picture was printed in several New York papers. I cut it out and taped it into my photo album. Above my head I'd drawn an arrow and written in big, bold letters, ME.

I was nine years old when my father brought me to New Orleans for the first time. I don't remember where we stayed, but I know it was in the French Quarter. I loved Bourbon Street: the music, the lights, the sidewalk performers. It seemed so taboo, so adult, dangerous but just slightly so, like a dirty Disneyland.

We went to visit the places of his youth, though many of them had disappeared. The streetcar he used to take to the First Baptist Church was gone; so was the two-story apartment building where he'd lived.

He was surprised to see Francis T. Nicholls's name still carved into the façade of his old school. Nicholls had been a governor of Louisiana in the late 1800s and was a well-known racist. In New Orleans, however, they never erase history.

I have pictures of us strolling the streets of the French Quarter, sitting on a stoop spooning gobs of cherry-colored ice into our mouths. We went to a cemetery to visit a famous witch's grave. The old headstone was freshly marked with white-chalk crosses left by those who still believed in her spells.

Somewhere on Bourbon Street we posed for a

picture dressed in period costumes—a sepia snapshot I still have to this day. (During the Civil War, my father's ancestors fought on the Confederate side, and my mother had relatives who'd been Union soldiers, so to me the Civil War had always been a battle between "mommy's side" and "daddy's side.") In the photo, I'm clutching a shotgun; he's in a Confederate uniform, his hand resting on a sword. I didn't see it then, but looking at the photo now, I see the fear in his eyes. He'd already had one heart attack, the year before. He must have known that his heart was weakened; perhaps he felt it with each beat. A year later he was dead.

Not long after we launch the boat in the Lower Ninth Ward, we pass by the body of a woman floating facedown behind a house. A few feet away, on a garage rooftop, sits a box of unopened MREs (Meals Ready to Eat), emergency food dropped from a chopper trying to help. A few blocks from the dead woman, we find the body of a man sprawled on top of a car. His corpse is swollen and discolored.

Nearby I see a large white dog sitting in a partially submerged tree. There are dogs everywhere—stranded on steps, barking at the boat, floating on suitcases in slicks of oil. I see a dog lying on something; it appears to be dead. I ask Chris, my cameraman, to get a tight shot of its face. Both of us get startled when the dog suddenly opens its eyes. Excited, I decide to wade over to it, to give it some clean water, but as soon as I step out of the boat, I sink to my chest. I'm wearing waders, but they go up only so far, and water pours into them, destroying the microphone transmitter attached to my waist. The dog is scared by the sudden movement, and swims off.

———————

The next day we are back in the boat, watching a Coast Guard helicopter prepare to pluck two people from their front porch. We shout at one another to steady the boat. The chopper's heavy rotors blow dirty water in our mouths, our eyes. The water is black, filled with gasoline and oil, human waste and human remains, the carcasses of countless animals.

A boat filled with rescuers from a nearby parish tries to signal the chopper that they can pick up the two people on the porch. The rescuers have no radio communication, however, and are invisible to the helicopter pilot above. They watch the Coast Guard diver being lowered into the water, shake their heads and motor on. There's no coordination, and they're angry.

We wait until the chopper flies off, then check the house to make sure no one else is there. Drenched with the filthy water, we motor back to dry land to rinse out our eyes and disinfect our skin.

None of us talks about what we've seen. We focus on how to put the story together, which pictures will work, which sound bites to use. I suppose it's easier that way. Each of us deals with the dead differently. Some don't look, pretending they're not there. Others get angry, sickened by what they see.

One day, I run into a paramedic who launches into a lecture about why corpses in water float (gases build up inside the body's cavities and get trapped) and why they sometimes develop post-mortem head injuries (they get knocked about by the water and debris). I must appear interested, because he describes in great detail how shoulder

muscles can rupture when a drowning person begins to convulse, and how coroners often find injuries to a victim's hands and fingertips, because
when they drown, they try to grab hold of something as they die.

"There was this one body, we called him Harry
the Swimmer," a soldier from the Eighty-second
Airborne tells me, shaking his head. "He was just
floating around, and every day we'd have to check
to find out where he'd floated to. Harry the Swimmer. We finally tied his shoelaces to a stop sign, so
he wouldn't float away."

I write it down, and it sounds callous and cruel,
but you can't judge until you've been out there,
day after day, in the heat and stench.

"You find yourself making weird jokes to stay
sane," the soldier tells me, embarrassed he's already said too much.

————————

At dusk on Sunday, I meet a young psychiatry resident from Tulane University. His name is Jeffrey
Rouse and he's been treating cops and first-respond-

ers at a makeshift clinic set up in the Sheraton Hotel by another doctor named Greg Henderson.

When the storm hit, Rouse got his family out, then came back to the city with bandages and medicine. He also brought his nine-millimeter Glock, which he still wears strapped to his waist.

"I was not coming back to this town without this," he says, putting his hand on the Glock. "I have a sworn oath to help. And the last thing I want to do is hurt somebody. But I had to get here to help."

Rouse is clearly exhausted, shaken by what he's seen, and what he hasn't. "Where was the help for the helpers?" he asks. "People have died when they didn't need to. If a psychiatrist has to come in on his own with a gun and a backpack to help, that's not a failure of an individual, that's a failure of the entire system.

"This is the only chance we get for a test run if something even more horrible happens or something as horrible happens with a nuclear device in this country. And we botched this one. We won't get a chance to botch it again."

There's plenty of blame to go around. What began as a natural disaster has become a man-made one. Nowhere is that clearer than at the New Orleans Convention Center.

"This is where hell opened its mouth," Dr. Greg Henderson says, standing on a garbage-strewn street outside the Convention Center one week after the storm. "You remember that scene in **Gone With the Wind,** after the battle of Atlanta, where they just pull back with all the bodies lying in the street? That's exactly what it looked like outside the Convention Center, the entire front of it was covered with people just lying there."

Dr. Henderson is a pathologist. He was in New Orleans for a conference at the Ritz Carlton Hotel when the storm struck. Rather than flee the city, he decided to stay and see if he could help. He approached several New Orleans police officers who told him there was no clinic for first-responders, so he decided to set one up in the Sheraton Hotel on Canal Street.

"We broke in with two officers to the Walgreen's drugstore," he tells me. "There was one broken into down in the French Quarter, and all of the foodstuffs had just been taken but a lot of the drugs had not been looted, so those police officers held the looters at gunpoint and handed me some

Hefty trashbags and said 'Okay, you got fifteen minutes, Doc.' So I went into the pharmacy with a flashlight and just opened the bags and just went down the shelves and pushed everything into the bag, just up and down for fifteen minutes and started handing them out, and that's how I started a pharmacy in the Sheraton."

Two days after Katrina hit, Henderson heard that conditions at the Convention Center were bad, so he went there, escorted by a New Orleans police officer, thinking he could join up with a medical team already there. When he got to the Convention Center, however, he discovered that there was no medical team there, just evacuees. Thousands of them.

"The smell was overwhelming," he says, walking with me through an unlocked door into the now-empty Convention Center. The smell is still revolting. The people were bused out on Saturday; it's now Monday, one week since the storm, but the garbage they left behind is still all around. Two small dogs abandoned inside bark nonstop.

"They were packed everywhere," Dr. Henderson says, "all the way out into the street, and pretty much on the other side of the street; it was just one mass of humanity. No air-conditioning, just people, crying and dying. Crying and dying."

The day of the storm, officials at the Superdome had told those fleeing the floodwaters to head to the Convention Center. They said that buses would soon arrive to take the evacuees out of the city. However, no buses arrived until the end of that week. The Convention Center was not really a shelter at all. There was no medical attention, and no police presence inside. At the Superdome, people were searched before entering; at the Convention Center, no one got searched.

"I'd be walking through this crowd with just a stethoscope," Dr. Henderson remembers. "I'm not sure if I was being more of a doctor or a priest, you know? Because there's not a hell of a lot you can do with people this sick with just a stethoscope. The best you can do is for the ones who are not that bad and are going to make it; you can put the stethoscope on their heart and hold their hand and say, 'Just hang on, just hang on. I promise something's coming.'"

"When you said that," I ask, "did you believe it?"

"I believed it somewhere in my heart. I just didn't know when it was going to happen," he says, looking around at the empty hall. "I knew they weren't going to leave us forever."

Dr. Henderson picks up a child's shoe, and a few tears run down his cheek.

"You had all these voices," Dr. Henderson recalls, "saying, 'Is there any help coming?' 'Doctor, I need you. Doctor, doctor, doctor, doctor, we're over here, over here.' What arose over the five days of anarchy, if you will, was just sort of a general lawlessness. I heard some pretty harrowing stories, and I think a lot of those stories got a lot of press and maybe contributed to this area not getting help. I think there was a collective attitude of everyone was just murdering everyone down there. 'Just stay away from that area or you're going to die.'"

I am silent while wandering through the deserted Convention Center with Dr. Henderson, stunned that this could have been allowed to happen, and that it took so long for relief to arrive.

Local, state, and federal officials had all seen models of what a storm of this magnitude would do to New Orleans. Hurricane Ivan, the year before, had come close. No one seemed to have adequately prepared for Katrina. Despite extensive television coverage, Michael Brown, the head of FEMA, didn't even know that people were stuck at the Convention Center until he was asked about it by reporters on Thursday.

"We look at each other with maybe too much hubris and say, 'This is America, this doesn't happen here,'" Dr. Henderson says, sitting with me amid a pile of rubbish on the curb outside the Convention Center. "This is disgraceful. This is a national disgrace. Nowhere in this country should that ever have to happen again. But unless we learn from this, it's going to be very ugly 'cause it's going to happen again."

My grandfather died in New Orleans. The year was 1944. My father was seventeen and had just graduated high school. He was working at Maison Blanche, a department store on Canal Street, selling young men's clothing. The store is gone, but the building remains. It's now the Ritz Carlton Hotel, where Dr. Henderson was staying when Katrina hit.

My grandfather came to New Orleans for a visit. One Friday evening he lay down on the sofa in the living room and fell asleep. He never woke up. My grandmother and my father's younger siblings went back immediately to Mississippi, but my father stayed to make funeral arrangements.

He'd never been close to his father. He feared

his quick temper, his unpredictable moods. When he wrote about him in his book, he described him as a "creature of charm, magnetism, tyranny, and madness."

My grandfather was not a religious man. He never went to church. "The Almighty knows about the people up at the church," he once told my father. "He doesn't know anything about me. When I die, I'll be no different from an old rotten limb falling off a tree and lying on the ground."

My father didn't know what to do with his father's body. He called the Lamana-Panno-Fallo Funeral Home. It was the only one he knew; he used to pass by it every day riding the streetcar.

When he went to collect his father's body from the funeral home, to take it to Mississippi for burial, he was surprised to discover that the morticians had laid him out beneath the outstretched arms of a large statue of the Virgin Mary.

"I don't know how they'd done it," my father later wrote, "but they'd turned him into an Italian. He looked exactly like an Italian banker. There was something excessively combed and waxy in his appearance, almost as if they'd stuck on a little black moustache. Clutched in his hands was a silver crucifix, an incongruity so astounding that I might have laughed if I had not had a watchful audience in Messrs. Lamana, Panno and Fallo, who were responsible for the comic outrage."

A silver crucifix would not have been well received in Meridian in those days, so my father asked for it to be removed before he took the body back to Mississippi for burial.

A few months after Katrina, I notice, in the **Times Picayune,** a funeral announcement for a woman whose body has recently been recovered. Her services are being held in the Lamana-Panno-Fallo Funeral Home. It turns out that they moved off St. Claude Avenue years ago, but are still in business near New Orleans. They weathered the storm, and are now helping its victims return home.

Aftermath

It's Tuesday, just over a week since the storm, and the floodwaters are receding, a bit more each day. Last week there were not enough police; now there are too many. Thousands of law enforcement personnel from all around the country have descended on New Orleans. The bodies, however, remain uncollected, and hundreds of residents are still trying to tough it out, refusing to leave their homes and their pets.

"This is a dog and pony show," a New Orleans cop says to me, laughing. "Twenty thousand law enforcement officers in the city right now, for what? Three thousand people? There are all these agencies with firepower meant for Iraq. I've got guys who I'm responsible to drive around and help patrol, and they're frustrated with me because they've got no action: 'We want some action, we want some action!' 'Well, you know, I'm sorry we can't provide any action for you so you can go out and play war games with your toys that you've never gotten to use.' It's a joke. It's way, way, way too much, way, way, way too late. It's like a big Mardi Gras parade of police, only there's nobody to catch any beads, 'cause there's nobody left out there."

FBI, FEMA, ICE, ATF, LAPD, ERT, NYPD—all the acronyms are here, and they all look the same: Oakley shades, narco-tactical vests, side-arms strapped to their legs. They stand around wearing T-shirts with steroid slogans, clutching high-caliber assault rifles, angled down, their index fingers at the ready.

Everyone wants to help, but there's just not much for them to do. I get stopped at a check-point by some National Guard troops. I show my ID, but one of the soldiers wants more.

"Do you have a letter from the battalion commander?" he asks me.

"I don't need a letter from the battalion commander," I say. He nods and waves me on.

"Nice going, Obi Wan," Neil Hallsworth, my cameraman, says to me. "We're not the droids you're looking for."

I'm not shocked anymore by the bodies, the blunders. You can't stay stunned forever. The anger doesn't go away, but it settles somewhere behind your heart; it deepens into resolve. I feel connected to what's around me, no longer just observing. I feel I am living it, breathing it. There is no hotel to go back to, isolated from the destruction, as there was in Sri Lanka. We are surrounded, all day, all night. There's no escape. I wouldn't want to get away even if I could. I don't check my voice mail for messages. I don't call home. I never want to leave.

We're sleeping in trailers parked on Canal Street, not far from the old Maison Blanche department store where my father worked. At night sometimes, when the broadcast is done, we sit outside the trailers in small groups, staring at the silhouettes of empty buildings. We don't need to say a thing. There is a bond that's forming among us. We are in new territory, on the cliff's edge. This place has no name, and all of us know it. The city is exposed: flesh and blood, muscle and bone. New Orleans is a fresh wound, sliced open by the shrapnel of a storm.

I'm not sure when it happened, when I realized that something had changed. I don't think there was a precise moment, a particular day. It's like when you're mourning and suddenly you become aware that the pain has faded. You don't remember exactly when it did. One day you laugh, and it shocks you. You forgot that your body could make such a sound.

Here, in New Orleans, the compartmentalization I've always maintained has fallen apart, been worn down by the weight of emotion, the power of memory. For so long I tried to separate myself from my past. I tried to move on, forget what I'd lost, but the truth is, none of it's ever gone away. The past is all around, and in New Orleans I can't pretend it's not.

When I was born, my parents lived in a five-story town house on New York's Upper East Side. Out front were two stone lions, silent sentinels guarding our home. There was a marble foyer and a sweeping spiral staircase, and though I don't remember the house well, I recall the smell of Rigo candles, green wax, heavy scent. The candles' flames shimmered against bottles of Noilly Prat, chilled Aquavit, and white wine in silver goblets with boar-tusk handles. There were fabric-draped walls, smooth silks, and needlepoint pillows, rough against a child's soft cheeks. The tables were laden with bowls of polished wood with piles of sterling silver fishes jumping out.

When my parents had parties, my brother and I were always encouraged to attend. I remember walking with my father through a smoke-filled room, my small hand safe in his. I craned my neck to see those around me, catching only brief flashes of faces and soft filtered light. There were powdered women with red lips, men in heavy shoes with thick hands and French cuffs. The rooms were filled with actors and artists, boldface names in society columns and kitchen conversations. Truman Capote was a frequent guest; his pudgy lisp made me giggle. Andy Warhol was there as well; his white hair scared me.

At a certain hour, my brother and I went upstairs to our room. We lay in bed in the dark listening to the laughter down below. There were hands clapping and glasses clinking, a muffled murmur that shook the floor. We closed our eyes as a piano played; a woman sang "Good Morning Heartache, my old friend..." Her distant voice lulled us to sleep.

I never imagined it was anything special. I never believed that that life would end. I had a father and a mother, a brother and a nanny, a childhood untouched by loss. When my father died, and the chasm first opened, it seemed easier just to run away.

After his death, we moved every few years—bigger apartments, one more beautiful than the last. My mother would get restless, start to redecorate. Then my brother and I knew it wouldn't be long before she'd begin searching for another home—a new place to settle, a new canvas to work on.

I didn't know my mother was famous until I was about twelve. I was in middle school when she designed a line of jeans that became wildly successful. On the street, suddenly people began to stare at us and point. My brother and I thought it was funny. We'd count how many times we saw our mother's name stitched on the back pocket of somebody's pants.

My mother once said that she survived the traumas of her childhood because she always felt that inside herself there was a crystal core, a diamond nothing could get at or scratch. I'd felt that same rock form inside me when my father died. In New Orleans, however, it started to crack.

Bourbon Street is closed, but a daiquiri bar has just opened. I think it's the first one. The entrance is boarded up, but through the heavy storm shutters you can hear the thumping bass of a stereo: Kelis sings, **"My milkshake brings all the boys to the yard / And they're like / It's better than yours..."** It's the first music I've heard since the hurricane.

To get in the daiquiri bar you have to go around back, through the lobby of the Royal Sonesta Hotel. The hotel's only just opened up as well, and we've moved in after a week in trailers. The FBI is staying there too; so are a bunch of New Orleans cops who no longer have homes.

Inside the bar is a wall of drinks in refrigerated coolers: Mango Madness, Citrus Storm, blood-red Hurricanes. The place is packed: reporters, police, FBI SWAT teams, a couple of drunk nurses.

Everyone's doing shots or drinking daiquiris and beer. There are more men than women, and the young cops are eyeing the nurses—horny, hungry, hoping to score.

Earlier in the day I ran into Dr. Phil McGraw. Some volunteers had set up a feeding kitchen for first-responders, and the **Dr. Phil Show** was there with a couple of cameras. The producer approached and asked if I wanted to speak with Dr. Phil.

"You mean as a therapist or as an interview subject for my show?" I asked.

"Either way." She shrugged.

The Scientologists are here too. Kirstie Alley arrived with a bunch of them, and John Travolta is around as well. No one beats Steven Seagal, though. He's not here with any group. I saw him late one night dressed in a cop uniform, out on patrol with some deputies from the Jefferson Parish Sheriff's Department. He's been going out with their SWAT team. We talk a bit, and when he leaves he puts his palms together in front of his face and bows briefly. Then he hops in a cop car and speeds off.

"Seagal's tight with the sheriff in Jefferson," a New Orleans cop tells me later. "There's a bar where a lot of cops hang out, and I remember a couple years ago Seagal comes in with those guys and takes out a framed eight-by-ten photo of himself and fucking hangs it on the wall."

"Get out of here," I say, "no way."

"I shit you not," he says. "As soon as he left, a couple of us took out our pistols and shot it. Blew the fucking thing off the wall. One bullet actually went right through and hit a car-rental place next door."

I don't really drink, but I like the bar because there's no bullshit here. For days the chief of police, Eddie Compass, has been blaming some of the problems the police faced after the storm on the fact that the armory got flooded and a lot of their ammunition and supplies were ruined. When I mention this to some of the cops at the bar, they burst out laughing.

"I'll take you to the fucking armory," one police officer tells me. "It's fucking empty. The police force is broke, and it was broke long before the storm."

A lot of the cops feel betrayed, screwed from above, below, and behind. They're pissed off that the media has been focusing so much on the police officers who didn't show up for work during the storm. I don't blame them. Out of a force of about 1,700 police, only some 120 were unaccounted for. The vast majority of cops came to work, and stayed on duty around the clock. They were barricaded inside their stations, working multiple shifts. Over at the Sixth District, the precinct headquarters was flooded, so the police set up a perimeter in the Wal-Mart parking lot. They chased the looters out, saved hundreds of guns from getting out on the street, and ended up sleeping in their cars for weeks.

I spend a couple hours at the Wal-Mart one night. The police have renamed it Fort Wal-Mart. I tell the cops there about the French Quarter police I met my first day here, who've renamed their precinct Fort Apache.

"Let me tell you something," the Sixth District commander, Captain Anthony Cannatella, tells me. "**We** are the original Fort Apache. Those guys over in the First District may be using the name, but this is Fort Apache."

We're sitting on benches with a half-dozen or so young cops, eating barbeque in the parking lot. Some police from Texas have come to help out, and every night they fire up the grill and barbecue whatever meat they can find. As he talks, Captain Cannatella's face is backlit; the electricity's still out, but a generator keeps a single light illuminating the area. Smoke swirls in the air.

"I don't know," I say, teasing. "They have a sign and everything—it says FORT APACHE—hanging right over the entrance to the precinct down there."

"We'll see about that," one of the police officers says, and a couple of guys get up and leave.

Captain Cannatella's been on the police force for more than twenty years. He is a big man with thick arms.

"You don't want to get slapped with one of those," a junior officer says, laughing, pointing to the captain's hands. Captain Cannatella clearly loves the men and women he commands, and I can tell they'd do anything for him.

"A lot of us older guys underestimated the young generation of police officers," he says, "but let me tell you, what these guys did here these last two weeks was extraordinary, and I would stand by any of them, any day."

About an hour later, as I'm getting ready to leave, a squad car pulls into the parking lot. Two young officers step out, one clutching the hand-drawn Fort Apache sign that up until a few minutes ago hung over the entrance to the First District's headquarters.

"How'd you get that?" I ask, laughing.

"We snuck right in there, crawled under the

Duty Officer's desk, and cut it free," one of the guys says, laughing. "Who's the real Fort Apache now, motherfucker?"

———————————

"I don't think I could ever come in and look at this place the same," Captain Casey Geist says. "I'll never come here for a football game."

We're in the Superdome. It's empty now, except for a few dozen cleaners in white hazmat suits scraping the grime off the seats and floor. It's noisy. Miniature tractors pick up the mounds of garbage piled on the Astroturf field. Here and there you find a child's football, abandoned wheelchairs, rotting food half eaten by evacuees. Some twenty thousand people took refuge in the Superdome, told to come by the city's mayor, who called it a shelter of last resort. He'd hoped that help would arrive from the state or federal government within two days. It didn't. Hope is not a plan.

Captain Geist is with the Eighty-second Airborne. He's been to Baghdad, but says that this is much worse. He's heard a lot of the rumors about what happened inside the Superdome, and he's not sure which of them are true. He seems to believe any of them is possible.

"People were here, they were doing drugs. People were having sex out on the floor, shooting up," he says, recounting the various stories he's heard. "It seemed like just madness, uncontrollable madness."

At the Superdome, however, there was at least some order. They had medical attention, stockpiles of food and water, and police and National Guard. When the levees failed, however, and the electricity with it, the Superdome started to bake. The mayor had warned people to bring their own food, and some did, but as the floodwaters spread, more people began arriving.

"They started defecating all over the place," Captain Geist says, shaking his head. "You know you can go to one corner, and everyone can go to the bathroom in one spot, but, I mean, people would drop their pants in the middle of the field and just go."

We like to think we are so advanced. We like to imagine we have protection from our own dark impulses. The truth is, it doesn't take much for all of that to be stripped away. Desperate people sometimes do terrible things. New Orleans was no different. The lights go out, the temperatures rise, and very quickly we get in touch with emotions that the cool air keeps at bay. We are all capable of anything. I've seen it again and again. Great compassion, terrible carnage—the choice is up to us.

Pretty soon they'll have finished cleaning up the Superdome, and the debris at the Convention Center will be swept away. It seems that a lot of people want the evidence, the memory, simply to disappear, the slate to be wiped clean. One day there will be football games played in the Superdome once again, and all of us will forget the lessons we've learned.

"Mark my words, man," a cop tells me one day, "it's all going to be cleaned up and forgotten. It's all going to be for shit. People are going to cover up things. And you know, these people are poor. No one's going to speak for them."

"You really think people will forget?" I ask.

"I've had family members tell me, 'Why don't you just leave, why don't you just leave? You didn't sign up for this.' But my father was at D-day, and what if he had said 'Forget it, I'm not doing this. I didn't sign up for this. There's too many people dying. There's too much carnage.' You just don't leave. You can't just forget."

I try not to imagine my brother hanging from the ledge. Try not to picture him pressed against the balcony, his legs dangling fourteen stories above the concrete sidewalk. Did a couple out for a summer stroll catch a glimpse of him before he let go? Did a family gathered around the dinner table see him plunge past their window? What was he thinking right before he hit the ground?

That's the thing about suicide. No matter how much you try to remember how that person lived his life, you can't forget how he ended it. It's like driving by a car smashed on the side of the road. You can't resist craning your neck to take stock of the damage.

"Will I ever feel again?"

That was the question my brother asked moments before he let go of the ledge he was hanging from. It didn't make sense to me at the time. I'd even forgotten he said it until my mother recently reminded me.

We both had tried to cauterize our pain, push our pasts behind us. If only I could have told him that he wasn't the only one. I abandoned him long before he abandoned me. I see that now. I could have reached out to him, talked with him, but he didn't make it easy, and I was a kid, and had myself to worry about.

Several months before he died, my brother went back to Quitman, Mississippi, back to our father's hometown. I didn't know it at the time. I found out only after his death. I went to his apartment and noticed a roll of film he'd never developed. The pictures were from his trip. My father's sister Annie Laurie was still living in Quitman at the time. Carter could have gone to visit her. He didn't. He simply wandered around the town. I realize now that in those last months of his life, he was searching for feeling, but he just couldn't reach out.

In every disaster I've ever been to, there's always been someone making money. Even in Somalia, some people got rich running guns, selling khat, providing security and cars to reporters. Who knows how many people continue to get rich off Iraq, with shady deals and crooked contracts? In

New Orleans, while parts of the city are still underwater, investors are already circling, looking for properties to buy up on the cheap.

"I've been doing real estate for twenty years, and I've never seen anything like it," Brandy Farris says, maneuvering her silver SUV through New Orleans' Garden District. "It's just crazy. We have a lot of investors calling; they're wanting to buy New Orleans property, wherever it is. They're buying them even underwater."

Farris is a broker with Century 21 in Baton Rouge, and she's come back to New Orleans for the first time to put FOR SALE signs up on some new listings. She has buyers in Miami, Seattle, and New York.

"They say, 'I want to buy land sight unseen.' If it's flooded they don't care. They did this with Hurricane Andrew—bought up all the properties that were flooded and they rebuilt the houses when it was time."

On her business card is a photo of Farris, long blond hair and a startling white Southern smile. In person she looks the same, except she wears a wireless cellphone headpiece attached to her ear at all times. Her phone seems to ring every few minutes.

"There are a lot of **ifs**," she says, momentarily

wrinkling her nose. "We have to assess what the damage is, see if we can even change title from the courthouse. We don't even have a way to file anything in the courthouse. A lot of people say their paperwork is underwater. They have no way to show who they are, what their mortgage is. We may just take purchase agreements and see what happens."

Her trunk is full of Century 21 signs attached to stakes, which she hammers into what remains of some people's yards. She also has another sign with her name on it and her commission—4 percent for a ninety-day listing.

"We're certainly not trying to take advantage of anyone losing their home," Farris says, concerned about how all this may look. "In any situation, you're always going to have the vulture investors, but there's something for everyone here. Rich, poor—investment, rentals. I hope it's going to be great."

We get out of the car and head toward a home she's just listed. Her high heels wobble precariously on the cobblestone street.

"Seriously, what is that smell?" she asks me.

"Probably a dead dog, maybe a person," I tell her.

"It's really bad. It's a lot worse than I thought," she says.

"Will the smell be a problem for buyers?" I ask.

"We're just going to have to take one case at a time," she tells me, not blinking an eye. "Everybody has a different need right now. It's very emotional. It's very traumatic."

In the past few weeks, Farris estimates, Century 21 has sold some 1,500 homes in Baton Rouge, a big rise from what the agency would normally sell—and prices are moving up. Farris is not sure what will happen in New Orleans, but she's positioned herself to benefit either way.

"I hope it's going to be great," she says, flashing the smile that's helped her sell many properties over the years. "President Bush says he's rebuilding New Orleans. We think it's going to be great. We're looking forward to it."

Brandy Farris is nothing if not optimistic.

It's two and a half weeks since the storm, and at the daiquiri bar the music is pumping. Outkast sings "Hey Ya." The bar is not very crowded, and for the first time I notice that white police officers sit on one side, African American officers on the other.

One of the cops I'm sitting with is angry at CNN. We aired a story about some police who were allegedly looting after the storm. He's not disputing that it happened, but he wishes we'd done more to point out that it was only a handful of cops.

The police officer has just had two days off. He drove out of state to visit his kids. He went in a police cruiser, which New Orleans cops are allowed to use on their days off. Every couple of hours, however, he was stopped by state police, who thought he was a deserter.

"The first cop who stopped me gave me a card with his name on it and his phone number, in case I got stopped again. But the next time it happened, they just ignored the card. They'd stop me and make me go through the whole explanation each time." Even their own seem to have turned on them.

Another cop, who's been on the force more than a dozen years, says he plans to leave. A few years ago he'd been offered a job with a small-town police force in the midwest, but turned them down. Now he says he's going to call them back. "I'll work anywhere. I don't care. I just want out."

"With 9/11 they treated it like a crime scene," he says, holding his beer by the neck. "With 9/11 they sifted through the wreckage, every piece. Here, they're simply going to bulldoze some of those buildings, which still have people in them. Months from now, people are going to be sitting around and they'll say, 'Yeah, whatever happened to old Joe. Where'd he go?' And no one will know. People will simply disappear."

His neighbor was dead for two weeks before anyone realized she was missing. "I went and found her body," he says, his voice clipped. "I took a forensics class a couple months ago, and they told us, in a situation like this, to always look for the flies. I actually found my neighbor by listening to the beating wings of flies."

Drinking with these police officers, I can't help but feel they're the only ones who'll really remember what happened here. I saw pieces of the horror; they saw it all—who was here, who wasn't. They know who the real heroes are.

A cop says, "You can tell, it's the people who do this"—with one hand he mimicks someone talking—"the people who are talking big, they are the ones who ran."

When the storm hit, his fiancée told him to leave. "'Fuck them,' she tells me, 'fuck the police,'" he says clutching a beer. There are nearly a dozen more on the table. "I told her, 'I was a cop before I met you, and I'll be a cop after you leave. Fuck you.'"

Like a lot of cops, he tried to look after family members while still doing his job. He used a wave runner to help rescue his partner's mom. As he took her out, he realized how many more people still needed help.

"We turned a corner, and there were just dozens of people on roofs, and they were all crying out. You could hear some of them trapped in their homes, all screaming. Just driving away, leaving them in the dark, that was the hardest part." His voice is quiet, plaintive. "I'm only twenty-three," he says.

In disasters, in war, it isn't governments that help people, at least not early on. It's individuals: policemen, doctors, strangers, people who stand up when others sit down. There were so many heroes in this storm, men and women who grabbed a bandage, an axe, a gun, and did what needed to be done.

Well past midnight, I stroll down Bourbon Street with a half-dozen cops. The street is empty and dark. The cops are off duty, out of uniform. A Louisiana state trooper pulls his car over and demands their IDs. He knows they're New Orleans police, but it's past curfew and he wants to prove a point.

"Fuck you," one of the police officers yells. "You're in my city, telling me I'm violating curfew? Fuck that." The trooper drives off. We walk back to the bar. There's no place else to go.

———————

Black Hawk helicopters still pass overhead, the sound crushing, comforting. The cavalry's come; help has arrived. They're still occasionally plucking people off rooftops and porches. Now it's the holdouts who decided to stay but have finally had enough.

Since the storm, the hallways at the Coast Guard command center at Air Station New Orleans have been crowded with cots—pilots and mechanics crashing between flights. Hundreds have come from all over the country, flying sparkling red choppers, angels from the sky.

Lieutenant Commander Tom Cooper flew the first rescue mission over New Orleans, hours after the storm. He joined the Coast Guard straight out of high school, and has been to a lot of disasters, but this one he'll never forget.

"Their images stay with you, you know?" he

says of the people he rescues, and I know exactly what he means. "You never get to talk to them because the helicopter's so loud. You hear them yell thank you every once in a while, but most of the communications is just done looking in their eyes.

"It's like an out-of-body experience, you know? to see that, to see it in person, to see it live—people crawling out of their attics on to their rooftops and signaling you for help."

Underneath the hovering chopper, the rotor blades create a mini-storm, hot air whips your face, water sprays all about. When he hovers, Cooper is unable to see the people below him. Normally he has a copilot, but there are so many missions that at times he flies alone. A flight mechanic squats behind him, helping him line up the helicopter. The mechanic holds onto a handle, controlling a hoist used to lower the Coast Guard diver. The diver is attached to a cable, and the hoist can lower him as much as two hundred feet.

The day after the storm, Cooper flew with Lieutenant Junior Grade Maria Roerick, who had just been certified as a Coast Guard pilot. It was her first rescue mission.

"Everywhere you'd look, you'd turn, there's

somebody over there, there's somebody over there," she remembers. "You had to start sorting people out, saying, 'There's kids,' or 'There's elderly. I think they need medical attention over there.'"

In the six days after Katrina, Coast Guard pilots out of Air Station New Orleans saved 6,471 lives—nearly twice as many as they'd saved here in the past fifty years combined.

When she sleeps, Roerick still sees the faces of people waiting to be rescued. "You go to bed at night completely exhausted," she says, "knowing there are still thousands of people out there. You can't get them all. You want to scoop them all up."

We wake each day unsure what lies ahead. Early in the morning, we gather in the lobby of the hotel. Few words are spoken before we head out. We climb into our SUV, a small platoon searching the city. The water recedes, new streets emerge, the map is redrawn every day.

Some residents still refuse to leave. On the street

outside her two-room rental, I spot an elderly lady, overweight, overtired. She sits on a rusty metal chair and leans on a cane with the words LOVE MINISTRIES crudely carved into the wood. She stares straight ahead, but her eyes are clouded and seem to be focused somewhere just above the horizon. Her name is Terry Davis, but she says around here everyone calls her Ms. Connie.

"I'm legally blind," she tells me, "and they won't let me take my service dog with me."

On the corner, Los Angeles police officers are fanning out, trying to get everyone on the block to leave. It's been three weeks since the storm, and the mayor has announced that everyone has to get out of the city. Forcible evacuations, some are calling it, but the truth is, they aren't really forcing people out.

"It's just temporary," a police officer says to Ms. Connie.

"No, no, dear," Ms. Connie says, slowly standing up. "I don't mean to be a hard case, but my dog goes where I go, or I don't go."

Normally, I wouldn't intervene—I'd just stand back and observe—but in this case it doesn't feel right. I've just talked to some National Guard troops who told me they have changed their policy and are now allowing people to take their pets on board the evacuation helicopters. I tell the police officer that the policy has changed. He goes back to talk with his superiors.

Ms. Connie lives alone with her dog, Abu. Her husband died years ago. Both he and Ms. Connie were traveling preachers. She invites me inside her home. In her living room there is a large hole in the corner of the ceiling, damage from Katrina.

"This is my skylight," Ms. Connie says, chuckling. Though legally blind, she can see just enough to move around, but not to clean. The apartment is a mess. A thick layer of dirt and dust covers everything.

"I don't trust law officials," she says. "They can't make up their minds." She isn't sure what she would pack if she were to leave, and she has nothing to pack her belongings in. The suitcase she used in her traveling days is broken. On the refrigerator is a hand-drawn sign in smudged ink: JESUS IS LORD.

"**I'm** not sure where I will end up," she tells me, "but **God** knows where I'll end up."

The police officer returns and tells Ms. Connie she can bring Abu along.

She believes it's a sign. The time has come to go. "I believe the Lord gives you guidance and will give you guidance, if you listen..."

"God is still watching over New Orleans?" I ask.

"Absolutely, absolutely," she says, smiling. "Will she rise again? Absolutely, absolutely."

An off-duty Hyatt hotel manager reeking of booze takes us on a late-night tour of his Shangri-la. The Hyatt is where the mayor and his staff were holed up throughout the storm. It's within running distance of the Superdome. Cleaning crews have been busy disinfecting the lobby. It looks immaculate. The smell of mold and garbage is nearly gone. The manager takes us on a ride to the top floor and opens up the Regency suites for us to see. The whole side of the building, the outer wall of glass, is gone. The hotel won't be back in business anytime soon.

"Do you want to see the phone where the mayor called the president from?" the manager asks, a plastic cup of beer in his hand.

"No, that's all right," I say, deciding it's time to call it a night.

"I can get you into the Superdome," he says.

"I've been there three times already. These soldiers and police are so disorganized. It won't be any problem."

"Thanks," I say, "but I've already been."

Back at the Royal Sonesta Hotel the booze has stopped flowing. I give a producer some cash and ask her to organize a beer run to Baton Rouge. Each night, we've been collecting around the empty hotel pool—small groups drinking, unwinding. It's quieter than at the daiquiri bar, and the crowd is mostly CNN personnel. The gatherings are important—a reminder to each of us that we're not here alone.

The hotel's power comes and goes. Tonight it's off; a fire in the electrical supply room has apparently shut it down.

"I guess we're back in crisis mode," a handyman says to me as he picks up a flashlight and casually strolls down the hall, his stooped stride anything but a sign of crisis mode.

I introduce myself to a man at the bar. He's a local resident who's been helping CNN crews get around town. He doesn't recognize me, and when I tell him my name, he seems surprised.

"I thought you must be some old geezer," he

says, merlot on his breath, Mardi Gras beads wrapped around the stem of his glass. "When people say your name, they shake."

"I doubt that's true," I say, laughing.

"No, really," he insists. "You have the power of a thousand bulldozers."

I leave the bar and go to my room. I can't get the image out of my head: a thousand bulldozers. I don't think it's true, of course. I don't like to think about my job that way. I've never paid much attention to the business of news—who is watching, how big the audience is, what time slot I am in. That information always seems to take away from the work. Katrina, however, is different. So many times in Africa I wanted people to know the suffering of others, but I long ago gave up believing that it would really change anything. Now people are watching, and I feel that maybe I **can** be of some help. I see it in people's eyes; they talk to me on the street: "Hey, Anderson, somebody's got to do something about what's happening over in St. Bernard," they'll say. Or: "You gotta do something about the bodies. Why aren't they being picked up?" I don't want to let these people down, this city, down.

I worry I've forgotten what's important about my brother, what's not. I recall looks, images, arguments. There was the time Carter punched me when I was an infant. The time in high school when he screamed at me, "You're not my fucking father!" and stormed out of my room. The day I scrawled, "I HATE HIM!" in a diary.

"Were you close?" Inevitably I get that question. Sometimes it's right after a person finds out about my brother's death; sometimes it's only after weeks of their knowing me. Were we close? Not so close that I knew he was going to kill himself. Not so close that I understood why he did.

I knew his laugh, his smell. I knew the sound he made when he walked through our front door, the jingle of his keys, the particular way his shoes scraped on the floor. We didn't talk, however. I didn't ask him deep, probing questions. Do any brothers do that sort of thing? I knew what I observed, I knew his surface, but clearly that was not enough.

I still dream about him, and in my sleep he seems so real. They're not happy dreams, however, because I know he's going to kill himself, and there's nothing I can do to stop him. I wake up believing for a moment that he's alive. I wake up filled with dread.

I found a Polaroid of my mom, Carter, and me celebrating his birthday. It was the first one after my father's death. The cake is small and has twelve white candles almost a foot and a half in length. Carter bends sideways in a half hug with our mom. She's smiling, and I'm next to her. I find these photos from time to time—frozen moments, I can't remember. Every time I do, the violence of Carter's death shocks me again. I keep the pictures, as well as his scribbled notes and magazines—the things I found in his apartment. I tell myself that one day I'll go through them and perhaps discover some clue that will help me understand, help me answer that question: Were we close?

"Them bodies smell like some stanky ass pussy," a Border Patrol agent tells me. Behind him a stripper in a cop's uniform hangs upside down from a pole. "That shit gets in your clothes, you can't get the smell out. Goddamn stanky ass pussy."

We're in Déjà Vu, the first strip club to reopen in New Orleans. It's just over three weeks since the storm. Beneath some colored lights, a handful of girls bump and grind on the bar, rubbing their breasts in patrons' faces. The place is filled with the storm's flotsam and jetsam: cops and soldiers, National Guard, Border Patrol, Customs—you name it, they're all here, their badges and guns badly concealed. They're clutching dollar bills, horny as hell and twice as bored.

I'm here to meet a New Orleans police officer, but he's not around. I call him on his cellphone, and he answers in the middle of a fight. "Fuck you, get the fuck out of here!" he yells to someone, then, finally tells me, "Anderson, I gotta call you back." A few minutes later, he's in the bar, apologizing.

"This National Guard guy took my seat when I went to the bathroom," he says. "When I get back, I tell him, 'That's my seat,' and he tells me, 'Fuck off.' Fuck off? He's with the National Guard. What the fuck is that? I'm the PO-leese. So I grabbed him and took him outside. Bullshit."

The night grinds on. Buying beers and whisky shots, the cops come and go, off duty, tired. Their wives and girlfriends are gone; they have no homes to go back to.

"You gotta do something," one cop tells me, inches from my face. It's late, everyone is drunk, the stripper's G-string is filled with wet bills. "No one gives a shit," the police officer tells me, tears streaming down his face.

Earlier, the police were asked to pass a hat for a fellow officer shot in the head during the looting. He's in a hospital in Houston; the money is for his family.

"You can't let them forget. We're counting on you," he tells me. The stripper finishes her set, and another takes the stage.

"I love you, man," one cop tells me. He doesn't mean it, of course, but right now he thinks he does. They've been screwed and abandoned, and I'm buying the rounds.

———

Every politician I talk to seems to say the same thing: "Now is not the time to point fingers." Spin doctors even come up with the term **blame game.** "I'm not going to play the blame game," they say, dismissing you when you ask for answers, for the names of officials who made key decisions. I notice that some reporters start using the term too. I can't understand why.

Demanding accountability is no game, and there's nothing wrong with trying to understand who made mistakes, who failed. If no one is held accountable for their decisions, for their actions, all of this will happen again. Not one person has yet to stand up and admit wrongdoing. No politician, no bureaucrat, has admitted a specific mistake. Some have made blanket statements, saying they accept responsibility for whatever went wrong. But that's not good enough. We need to know specifics. What was done wrong? What were the mistakes?

I ask any official I can. No one will answer. The only "mistakes" they admit to are actually veiled criticisms of others. The mayor should have declared a mandatory evacuation on Saturday, instead of waiting until Sunday. Precious hours were lost. The governor could have done that as well, but didn't. They could have moved hundreds of city buses and local school buses to higher ground and used them to evacuate the nearly one hundred thousand residents who had no access to private transportation. They didn't. There were plenty of mistakes to go around. I just want someone to admit to them.

The mayor announces a plan to repopulate the city, but three days later after heavy criticism, he backs off, blaming Hurricane Rita. Rita is on the cusp of becoming a category 3 storm, and it's heading this way. It's projected to make landfall around Galveston, Texas, and already the media is gearing up, pulling out, like children drawn by shiny objects.

After weeks of asking, the mayor finally agrees to an interview with me, but after it's done, I feel as if I blew it. We spoke a lot about Rita, because it was in the headlines, but I wish I'd focused more on Katrina mistakes. I worry that politicians are trying to divert attention away from the failures, to delay and distract people until they forget.

At the end of the interview I ask the mayor if he'd be willing to come back on again and discuss what he did wrong and what others did wrong. He says he would be happy for the opportunity. For the next four months, however, he declines my every invitation to sit down and talk.

Over the phone my producers are telling me that I'm doing great. Each day they tell me the ratings for my broadcast are high, but the truth is, I don't want to hear about it. This is not a "story"; these people aren't characters. It doesn't feel right to talk about plot lines and rating points.

At times I feel like a failure, as if I'm not up to the responsibility. At night, when I try to sleep, I go over the questions I've asked interview subjects, the wording, the accuracy. Did I stutter and stammer and beat around the bush? Was I fair? Was I too emotional? Did I give the guest a chance to answer? Did I let him ramble on too much? Did I get spun? I worry that our cameras are not capturing enough. I'm not sure it will ever be possible to capture it all.

I head to Texas, for Hurricane Rita, and when I come back to New Orleans, I notice a change. I see the number of TV stories about Katrina start to lessen. I can feel the viewers' interest ebbing. As the floodwaters drop, the tide is slowly turning. It's the fourth week since the storm, and I suppose it's inevitable, but when it happens it still comes as a shock: Each morning we ask ourselves, "What can we do that's new? What haven't we seen?"

"We haven't seen enough," is all I can answer. My mind is racing; at times I feel manic. My thoughts jump from one to another: make sure the audio in the cop interview I just did is usable; cancel this month's appointments; call Mom; check on the dog; track down names of wounded police officers. The list scrolls endlessly in my head.

I don't want to go back to New York, to my job, to the way it used to be. Stories about missing co-eds in Aruba and runaway brides, stories that titillate but aren't as important. I talk to friends on the phone but don't have much to say. I want to yell at them, "Don't move on! Don't go back to your normal life, get caught up in the petty falseness you see on TV!" It's the same feeling I had weeks after my brother died. I was back at school, and everyone else seemed to have forgotten.

Martha Stewart has a new TV show starting. I see her picture in **USA Today.** I take it as an omen, a sign that the country has moved on. In the French Quarter a broken newspaper machine still holds the last edition of **USA Today** to hit the stands before Katrina hit. Martha Stewart's smiling face is on the front page. We're back to where we were before the storm. I've started to believe in signs and magical thinking. If I tie my shoes in the next ten seconds, people will still care about the story. If I make it through this intersection without having to slow down, I can stay here another week.

I realize I've been dehumanizing the dead, calling them "corpses" or "bodies." I should be ashamed of myself. They're our neighbors, our country-men. They're people, and they deserve better care. I can't understand why it's taking so long to re-trieve them. FEMA announces that when they start to collect the people who have died, they won't allow us to videotape it. They say it's to pre-serve the dignity of the dead. I don't believe what they say anymore. I'm convinced that they want to cover up the horror of what's happened. If they were so concerned with dignity, they would not have tied the bodies of storm victims to stop signs so they wouldn't float away; they would not have let them lie out for so long uncollected, uncared for. We are not going to take pictures of storm vic-tims' faces. We are not going to be responsible for someone seeing a loved one's body on TV. But America should see the conditions our country-men have been left out in. If anything, covering up what really happened to them is what will deny them their dignity. CNN decides to sue to be al-lowed to videotape the body recoveries, and the case is settled. We are allowed to videotape, but when the recoveries actually begin, emergency workers on the ground often make it difficult for us to get a picture. They position their vehicles to block the shots.

"All I can say is there better be an independent investigation," a police officer says to me on a street in the French Quarter. I've never met him before, but he clearly wants to talk about what he's seen. It's past midnight, and he's been waiting for half an hour for me to finish my broadcast.

"They're hoping people will forget," he says, looking around to make sure no one sees him talking to me. "Honestly, I've forgotten things from five days ago. So the farther you get from an incident, the fuzzier the facts get. And that's all I can think of that they're hoping to do. I want to know why the governor rejected help that could've come. I want to know why the governor and the mayor, who I think is a good man, and the police chief, who I think is a good man, did not have a cohesive plan. It breaks me to say this because I love my department and I love my city—and I don't want to say anything bad about my chief—but something should've been put into place. There was no plan in place whatsoever."

We arrange to meet back at my hotel. He doesn't want his name used.

"I don't want to point fingers," he says, settling into a chair in a darkened room. "I'm just a patrolman, but nothing was prepared, and lack of organization and planning cost people their lives."

"Officials say no one could have predicted this would be so bad," I say.

"Well, the Hurricane Center knew what was going on. FEMA knew what was going on. Everybody knew what happened if the big one came to New Orleans. It came, we knew it was coming, we had plenty of warning, and people were told, 'Hold on, we can handle it ourselves. Hold on, we can handle it ourselves.'"

He pauses as tears fall down his face. "The people I swore I'd serve and protect—they're floating. They're dead. I didn't sign up for this. I didn't sign up to be abandoned. These are American citizens dying. This is not Ghana. This is not Burundi. These are not Hutus and Tutsis, or whatever, you know? They are American citizens. Old people were left in nursing homes to die."

He doesn't pretend to know exactly what went

wrong, what happened, but he's pretty sure race had something to do with it.

"I hate to go there, 'cause I'm white, but how can you not think race played a role?" he says. "If this was Governor Blanco's sisters and brothers dying here, do you think she can say, 'Forget it. We can handle it'? 'Give us twenty-four more hours, we'll figure it out.' I mean there were buses here, there were things we could've done to save those people. And they died in the hundreds, because nobody had an idea what to do. If this was a city in Connecticut, these people wouldn't have died.

"Man, all I can pray is an independent commission comes in and looks at what happened. Whether or not there are criminal charges, at least the public knows who to vote for next time. The poor planning caused a lot of people to die. There was no plan, there was no plan."

After a month, I reluctantly leave New Orleans. I head back to Mississippi for several days. John Grisham and his wife have begun raising money for rebuilding the Gulf, and they agree to meet me in Biloxi so I can report on their efforts. He suggests we meet at a restaurant called Mary Mahoney's. It's a Biloxi landmark that Grisham has included in several of his most popular books. Mary Mahoney's was badly flooded during the storm, and workmen are busy trying to get it reopened. I arrive before the Grishams, and when I walk into the restaurant, the owner, Bob Mahoney, smiles and says, "Welcome back."

"What do you mean 'welcome back'?" I ask.

"You came here with your daddy in 1976. He was on a book tour, and you'd just been at the waterslide park. You came in. You were still wet, wearing shorts and wrapped in a towel."

As soon as he mentions it, I remember the trip, the waterslide park; I was shivering, but didn't want to leave the clear blue water, I kept prolonging getting out. A friend of my father's had taken me to the park, and afterward brought me to the restaurant. I remember riding in her car, the feeling of my wet shorts on the vinyl seat, the clicking of the turn signal as we pulled into the restaurant's parking lot. I walked through the crowd to the table where my father sat. I remember the feeling of being with him so far away from home. Just he and I, two men on our own.

Bob takes me through a series of rooms and points out a large round table. "That's the table y'all sat at," he says, smiling. "It survived the storm."

"How did you remember all this?" I ask him.

"Mother was a big fan of fashion and writing," he says, pointing to a painting of his mother, Mary Mahoney, the restaurant's founder. "When Wyatt Cooper came into your restaurant in 1976, that was a pretty big deal."

I went to hear my father speak to a crowd of ladies in Biloxi. His book had just come out. He spoke to them of families and memories; he connected with them right away. At night we slept in the same hotel room, and he worked in the bathroom writing his speeches, with the door closed so the light wouldn't keep me up. I can almost remember the feeling, the safety. After he died, nothing ever felt safe again.

In Waveland, not much is different. The urban search-and-rescue team from Virginia with whom I spent time has just pulled out. More roads have been cleared, but that just makes it easier to see the devastation. A handful of work crews pick up downed trees and try to restore power lines.

I head over to the house where a month ago they found the bodies of Edgar and Christina Bane and their two sons, Carl and Edgar Junior. When I arrive, there are two cars parked outside. It turns out that Christina and Edgar Bane also had two daughters, Laura and Serena. They didn't live at their parents' house, and both survived the storm. They've come back to visit because yesterday was their mother's birthday. She would have been forty-five years old.

"A couple days after the storm, we came back," Laura Bane tells me, standing in what used to be the kitchen of her parents' home. "When I first turned the corner, I was all excited because the house looked untouched—no shingles missing or anything. As soon as I pulled into the driveway, I seen they had some writing on the door. They had a **V** with a circle around it. And underneath it, it had FOUR DEAD. So that's kind of when I just went crazy."

The writing on the door is barely visible now.

Laura is twenty-five but already seems much older. Her hair is pulled back tight into a ponytail and there's a blurred blue teardrop tattooed under her left eye. She has three kids and another on the way. Her sister, Serena, is eighteen and has the awkward posture of a girl not yet a woman. She already has a child, though, a little girl who is wandering around outside. Serena clutches a photograph taken in May at her high school graduation. She found it in her boyfriend's car. It's the only photo she has left of her mom.

Christina Bane's ashes are now in an urn in the apartment where Serena is staying. "At night my daughter, she'll go and she'll kiss the urn and she'll be like, 'Night-night,'" Serena says. "I don't know what I'm supposed to tell her. I never thought I'd have to do any of this. I'm eighteen. I never thought my parents would die when I'm eighteen. They were so young."

In honor of their mother's birthday, Serena and Laura had planned to barbecue today on the dried-out lawn of their parents' house, but the stench is still too great.

"My dad was right there next to the sink," Laura says, unaware that I saw his body there one month before. I try to tell her, but I don't think she understands. "The coroner did tell me that the refrigerator was in the middle of the living room floor, like right below the fan. And they had prints—like, feet prints—right inside the refrigerator, like they tried to get up to the attic. But the water was above the attic. So even if they did get into the attic, they wouldn't have survived."

For a moment I'm reminded of searching my brother's apartment after his death. I was looking for clues that might explain what happened. I was hoping to reconstruct events, build a time line. In the end it wasn't possible.

"I do try to imagine how it went, like step by step," Laura says. "I guess the water came in real fast, and they probably just panicked. My mom, she was the only one who knew how to swim. I think she could've saved herself but she didn't because she wasn't going to be able to save my brothers and my dad. So she just went with them."

"She'd been married to my dad for twenty-five years," Serena says softly. "There was no way she would have left them."

The Banes' bodies lay in their house for five days. During that time someone tried to steal Christina Bane's van from the driveway.

The house has now been stripped, the wallboard and insulation removed, the flooring cleared. All that remains is the wood frame and the exterior walls.

"The insurance man came today and he said he

doubts they could help, except for just little pieces of shingles that are missing off the roof. My parents didn't have flood insurance," Laura says.

Laura is living in a hotel room with her three children. She has until tomorrow to get out. Serena is staying at a friend's apartment with eight other people. They've applied for a FEMA trailer but are still waiting to hear back.

"Before I go to sleep I'll pray and I'll talk to her," Laura says of her mom, "and I can just feel them just hover over me. I think they want me to know that they're okay."

Serena is unsure what she is going to do. She still finds it hard to believe her mother is dead.

"If you needed anything, all you had to do was say, 'Mom, I need this,' and my mom would be at my house with it," she says, crying. "And now it's like, if I need something, who do I call?"

I sign off from Waveland, Mississippi. Tomorrow I'll return home. My office is insisting I come back, "at least for a little while." That's what they say, but I know it means it's over. They'll let me return, visit from time to time, do updates, but soon there will be other headlines, other dramas, and those who weren't here will want to move on.

When the final broadcast is done, we're standing on a destroyed street. There are about a dozen of us—producers and cameramen, engineers and satellite truck operators. It's near midnight. No one else is around. All the homes have crumbled. Everything is black, silent. We break down the equipment, wrap up the cables, and turn out the lights. Neil Hallsworth, one of my cameramen, takes out some beers from the cooler in his truck and passes them around. Someone cranks the radio on the dashboard of one of the rented SUVs. The Talking Heads echo in the dark.

"Into the blue again / after the money's gone / Once in a lifetime / water flowing underground." Bottles are opened, glass clinks against glass. "Nice job." Awkward handshakes. A few hugs. We promise to exchange photos. Some talk of other trips. The spell is quickly broken.

We pile into our SUVs and head in different directions: Baton Rouge, New Orleans, Biloxi, Mobile. Taillights grow distant. The promises won't be kept, the names remembered, or the photos sent. Memories will fade until the next time the storm bears down, the edge appears, and we rush to reassemble—a small band, knockabout boys, battle-scarred and full of what we've seen.

We are survivors, lucky and happy to be alive. It seems inappropriate against this backdrop of destruction. My muscles are taut, my mind wound tight. I'm ready to spring. I want to cry. I want to shout. All I can do is laugh. For a moment I'm back in Sarajevo, tumbling down Mount Igman, howling with my driver after exposing ourselves to snipers.

Driving through deserted streets, the SUV's headlights shine on splintered wood and collapsed homes. I don't want to leave these colorless streets, the mud and debris, cars hanging from trees. I don't want to return to the cleanness, the convenience, the traffic rules. I want the roadblocks, the hassles, the heartache, the look in peoples' eyes— thankful you're there. There is no good that comes from the storm, no silver lining, no Hollywood ending. Death descends. Lives are lost. No good comes of it, but you meet good people along the way. They open up their homes, they cook you food, give you a cot to crash on. I was honored to be here, privileged to have been a witness to so much feeling, so much kindness, so much heroism.

Back home it's petty, small—morning meetings

and celebrity stand-ups. The clicking and clacking of tongues. Freshly scrubbed faces. It's hard to imagine going back to that. I turn on the radio, searching for news, another spot on the map to head for. Baghdad is heating up, there are wild-fires in California. Maybe the storm has touched down again, maybe I will be in motion soon. The map of the world constantly changes, new fault lines split open, new frontlines appear. I want to hurl myself into the storm.

It's impossible to maintain, impossible to sustain. You can't stay like this forever. Blissed out. Bugged out. High, but not stoned. I'm in this moment. This second. Nowhere else. The work is done.

On the highway a few red embers glow on the horizon. I press down on the gas pedal and imagine myself dissolving into the dark, exploding into molecules transmitted through the air, floating forever in silent space—surrounded by potential, never having to slow down, never having to land.

Epilogue

In Oaxaca, Mexico, there is a celebration called el Dios de la Muerte, the Day of the Dead. It takes place every year on Halloween, the day when the souls of the dead are said to return for a few hours to the world of the living. On the night of October 31, Oaxaca's cemeteries fill with people who've come to welcome back their lost loved ones. They place candles around the graves and bring offerings of food and drink to help the dead sample the material world they've left behind.

I've come to Oaxaca because I wasn't sure where else to go. When I returned to New York from Waveland, I was told to take some time off, a couple of days at least.

"Go to a beach. Relax," someone suggested. The idea seemed impossible to entertain. I couldn't imagine lying on a beach, watching people sunbathe and swim in the surf. I feel as if I'm carrying with me all those I met and saw this year. I want to be someplace where they will be welcome.

I spend most of the week in Oaxaca sleeping and writing the beginnings of this book, but on Halloween night I head to the city's largest cemetery.

Oaxacans believe that the souls of infants come back first, and at their graves there is only sadness. At one child's headstone, I watch an elderly woman relight candles that keep blowing out in the wind. She's all alone. Parents of children tell no stories about their babies. The joy of their birth makes their sudden death that much harder to bear. At older people's graves, however, there is drinking and laughter. Funny tales about moments they shared.

Around one candlelit grave, I count nearly a dozen men standing shoulder to shoulder. They play some guitars and sing out of tune. Some clutch glasses of beer. One of the men is far drunker than the rest, and he hangs on the shoulders of his friends, weeping while they sing. Later I see him sprawled on top of another grave. His arms stretch out, he shouts at the stars.

I imagine all those whose stories I've told this year returning to their loved ones: Sunera and

Jinandari, Aminu and Habu, Christina and Edgar Bane, with Carl and Edgar Junior. I think about the people whose names I don't even know, whose bodies I saw abandoned or buried in unmarked graves. Who would be there to welcome them back?

I picture my own small family sitting around the graves of my father and brother. I suppose it would be just my mother and I. How would I welcome them back to the world of the living? What would I say? I've told their stories. I've kept them close. It's not enough, but it's all I was capable of.

I still wish I knew what my brother was thinking when he put his feet over the balcony outside my room. It's doubtful I ever will. He was a young man who wanted to be in control. In the end, he simply wasn't.

For so long I've been isolated by sadness; by the end of this year, however, I finally feel whole—connected to both the past and the present, the living and the lost. The world has many edges, and all of us dangle from them by a very delicate thread. The key is not to let go.

By midnight, Oaxaca's cemeteries are crowded. The dirt paths have turned to mud. Children dressed as skeletons and ghouls run amid the graves, asking for candy or trying to scare people passing by. There is so much laughter, even in the midst of all this loss. It's the way it should be—no distance between the living and the dead. Their stories are remembered, their spirits embraced.

Author's Note

The great majority of quotes in this book are from taped interviews I conducted. Those that are not are based on notes and journals I've kept over the years. There are no composite characters, no made-up stories. Memory is fallible, and in some cases my notes were not as detailed as I would have liked. Some dates may be off by a few days here or there, but I have gone to great lengths to ensure that this book is factually correct.

Acknowledgments

I have been writing much of this book in my head for years, but I would not have committed to actually putting the words on paper were it not for the encouragement of my literary agent and childhood friend Luke Janklow, and Dan Peres, who first asked me to write for **Details** magazine. I owe them both a debt of gratitude.

Jonathan Burnham and Tim Duggan have been remarkable editors, and I am grateful for their enthusiasm and insight. I'd also like to thank Jenna Dolan for doing such a careful copyediting job. Writing may be a solitary effort, reporting for television, however, is not, and over the years I've been lucky to work with a number of very talented producers from whom I've learned a great deal—in particular, I'd like to thank David Neuman,

Mitchell Koss, Jim Gerety, Kathy Christensen, Jon Klein, David Doss, Charlie Moore, Kathleen Friery, and Andy Court. I am also thankful for the counsel and kindness of my friend and agent Carol Cooper, who believed in me when many others seemed not to, and Jeff Young who has helped me more than I can ever say.

I would also not be the person I am today were it not for May McLinden and Nora Marley. Their selfless devotion over the years is impossible to quantify or ever adequately thank them for. I'd also like to acknowledge my good friends who helped me during the writing of this book. I'd like to thank Julio for his support and calm counsel without which this book would not have been possible. I'd also like to thank Steve, Andrea, and Kirk for reading advance copies and giving me their honest opinions. Finally, over the years I have been welcomed into many people's homes and lives. They've trusted me with their stories, and I am extraordinarily grateful for that.

PHOTO INSERT CAPTIONS

1. My brother and I, circa 1969. While I was still in my mother's womb, Carter labeled me "Baby Napoleon," but he was the true leader of our childhood campaigns.

2. This portrait of me was taken by my father, Wyatt Cooper. I was about eight years old.

3. On a trip to Quitman, Mississippi, in 1976. My father wanted us to understand and appreciate the shared soil in our blood.

4. My father in 1963, around the time he met my mother. As a child, I never saw the resemblance between us; now I look at pictures of my father and I see my face.

5. Carter at sixteen. After my father's death, both of us retreated into separate parts of ourselves, and I don't think we ever truly reached out to each other again.

6. Christmas, 1986: My mother, Gloria Vanderbilt, Carter, and I.

7. Posing with a Pygmy chief in Zaire, 1985. I was seventeen and had left high school a semester early. Africa became a place I'd go to forget and be forgotten in.

8. Moments after landing at the Sarajevo airport in Bosnia, 1993. I'm wearing a Kevlar vest and helmet for the first time. After a few days, however, I rarely put them on.

9. Working out of a destroyed beachfront hotel in Sri Lanka, January 2005. Christmas decorations still hang from the lobby ceiling. [Brent Stirton/Getty Images for CNN]

10. Searching for the bodies of two children, Jinandari and Sunera, in a hospital morgue in Sri Lanka, January 2005. [Brent Stirton/Getty Images for CNN]

11. Children training to become monks on a beach near Kamburugamuwa, Sri Lanka, January 2005. [Brent Stirton/Getty Images for CNN]

12. Early morning at a U.S. military checkpoint, Baquba, Iraq, December 2005. [Thomas Evans]

13. In Maradi, Niger. During the summer of 2005, 3.5 million Nigeriens were at risk of starvation. These kids were some of the lucky ones not suffering from malnutrition. [Radhika Chalasani/Getty Images for CNN]

14. Writing in my hotel room in Maradi. We end up working around the clock. Shooting all day, writing and editing stories well into the night. [Radhika Chalasani/Getty Images for CNN]

15. Broadcasting from a flooded highway on-ramp in New Orleans, September 2005. [Radhika Chalasani/Getty Images for CNN]

16. Beaumont, Texas, September 2005. Hurricane Rita arrives on shore. [Jensen Walker/Getty Images for CNN]